The Legend of Ararat

by the same author

Memed, my Hawk
The Wind from the Plain
Anatolian Tales
They Burn the Thistles
Iron Earth, Copper Sky

YASHAR KEMAL

The Legend of Ararat

Translated from the Turkish by
Thilda Kemal

Illustrated by Abidin Dino

COLLINS AND HARVILL PRESS
London 1975

This book was first published under the title of
AGRIDAGI EFSANESI by Cem Yayinevi, Istanbul

ISBN 00 261451 0
Set in Monotype Baskerville
Made and Printed in Great Britain by
William Collins Sons & Co. Ltd, Glasgow
for Collins, St James's Place, and Harvill Press,
30A Pavilion Road, London, SW1

The Legend of Ararat

A view of Mahmut Khan's castle at the foot of Mount Ararat

On the slopes of Mount Ararat, twelve thousand feet up, there is a lake called Küp Lake, Jar Lake, for it is no bigger than a threshing-floor, and very deep. In fact, it is more like a well than a lake. It is surrounded by jagged red rocks. A stretch of soft copper-coloured earth, which narrows as it leads down from the rocks to the lake, has been worn into clearly-marked tracks. There are some patches of fresh green grass on the copper-coloured earth. Then the blue of the lake begins. It is a blue unlike that of any other piece of water: a soft, velvety lapis-lazuli.

Each year when the snows melt and the earth awakens and the freshness of spring bursts forth on Mount Ararat, the shores of the lake, above the thin traces of snow, are full of tiny, fragrant, brightly-coloured flowers. Even the smallest of them, blue, red, yellow or mauve, can be seen from afar as a spot of blazing colour.

Every year when spring comes to the mountain, with its bright, fragrant flowers, the strong, handsome, sad-eyed, slim-fingered shepherds of Ararat gather at Lake Küp with their pipes. They cast their felt cloaks down on the ancient, copper-coloured earth at the foot of the red crags, and sit in a ring round the lake. Long before day-break, when the dazzling stars that crown Mount Ararat are still shining, they draw their pipes from their waist-bands and begin to play the tune that expresses the wrath of Ararat.

All day long they play, till sundown. Then at the close

7

of the day a tiny snow-white bird, long and slim, like a swallow, comes circling over the lake. Its flight is so swift that it traces one long white loop after another. As the white circles are seen against the deep blue of the lake, and the sun sinks in the west, the shepherds cease their piping. They put their pipes back into their waistbands, and as they rise the bird flashes down over the lake, dips one of its wings into the blue water and darts up again. Three times it dips its wings, then flies away and is lost to sight. After the white bird has gone, the shepherds withdraw silently, one by one, and disappear into the darkness.

A white horse had been standing at Ahmet's door all night long. It stretched out its neck and seemed to be sniffing with wide nostrils at the cracked wood of the door. Old Sofi was the first to see it. On its back was a silver-mounted Circassian saddle with stirrups of chased silver. The reins, slung over the gold nacre-embossed pommel of the saddle, were worked with silver. Beneath the saddle a decorated saddle-cloth of well-pressed felt extended down to the horse's rump. It was emblazoned with an ancient, bright orange sun-disk behind which rose a tree-of-life emblem, very green. On the left flank of the horse were the same sun-disk, the same tree-of-life. Sofi had seen them somewhere before. A vague memory stirred in him. These must be the heraldic bearings of some distinguished tribe or clan.

Sofi stood still for a while, somewhat startled, somewhat surprised, and frightened too. Who could be the distinguished guest who had come to Ahmet's house? In vain he racked his brains, he could not recall of what clan or Bey or Pasha these were the bearings. But he was afraid. Such emblems were ill-omened. They came bringing fear and left fear in their wake. There was no one in these parts who could own a horse so richly caparisoned, and besides, Sofi knew the emblems of every clan for miles around.

It was spring and the thaw had set in over Mount Ararat. Below, the tips of the red rocks showed here and

9

there and yellow crocuses peeped out of the snow. Far in the distance a flight of cranes, strung out one after the other, streamed through the sky making for Lake Van.

From inside the house the strains of a pipe floated out into the chequered dawn. Ever since he could remember, Sofi had been familiar with the sound of this beautiful pipe. Ahmet's grandfather, Sultan Agha, used to play like that and so did his father, Resul. Not in all Ararat, nor perhaps in all the world, could anyone play on the pipe like the men of this house, and Sofi knew it well, for he himself was famous as a piper in the eastern lands from the Caucasus to Persia and beyond.

Sofi moved a little nearer and examined the emblem more closely. The horse, pricking up its ears, seemed to be listening to the sound of the pipe. It was an ancient mountain song Ahmet was playing, about the implacable wrath of Ararat. Old Sofi had taught this song to all the shepherds thereabouts.

The horse stretched out its neck towards the sound. So did Sofi . . . It was a long time since he had played or listened to this song. Think of it, a huge mountain breaking into terrible fury, and all conveyed in the sound of a pipe! Men are unfathomable, Sofi thought, and strange confused thoughts passed through his mind. To produce a gigantic raging mountain out of a slender pipe! As long as they live on this earth men will find out everything. They will learn the secret of the eagle in flight, of the ant's nest, of the birth of the moon and of the sun, and of their setting, of life and death, of darkness and light . . . They will find it all out . . . All but the mystery of man himself. Only that they will be powerless to discover.

In the sound of the pipe all the mountain moved. Its

gorges and avalanches, its frozen night and stars exploded. The moonlight burst forth. And the mountain marched on in all its awesome anger, sweating, panting, its breast heaving like that of a giant. Sofi could hear its breath deep deep down, a distant rumble coming from the bowels of the earth. Ahmet played on and the mountain's angry breathing swelled.

At such times Sofi would put his ear to the throbbing earth and listen. Ararat's anger mounted, its breath grew quicker and deeper, it heaved and shivered into pieces and bore down on the earth with all the weight of its fury. And then there was a sudden silence, a desolation. Mount Ararat had vanished, taking with it its birds and beasts, its people, its stars, its moon and sun, its blowing wind, its rain and snow, its flowers, leaving the world empty and forsaken, carrying away even the flocks of sloe-eyed gazelles that fill the deserts. The voice of the pipe was frozen on a long note of emptiness and desolation. And all at once, the world opened up again before Sofi's eyes with all its flowers and stars and scents, with its bright trout-filled streams, its gazelle-run desert. He saw the horse again, but changed. The sun-disk on its felt saddle-cloth came alive. The tree-of-life burst into bloom.

The pipe had stopped playing now. Over the peak of Ararat the sun appeared, the tip of a crimson tongue.

Sofi came to himself. He looked at the horse, then at the door. The horse lifted its head and looked at Sofi too with large sad eyes. A vague fear crept into Sofi's heart.

The unknown horse that came to stand at Ahmet's door

'Ahmet, Ahmet,' he called.

Ahmet recognized Sofi's voice. He rose and opened the door. 'Come in, uncle,' he said. Then he saw the horse and was taken aback. He looked at Sofi inquiringly.

'Who's your guest, Ahmet?' Sofi asked. 'May he come in peace and joy.'

'I have no guest,' Ahmet replied.

They both gazed at the horse.

Suddenly it moved away, circled the house once and came to a stop at the door again. It was a long wide-rumped horse with erect tapering ears. Raising its head it made as if to neigh, but no sound came.

Ahmet's house, which stood at the foot of a rock, was built of unhewn red stones. It had a wide door and a single window.

Sofi was thinking. Ahmet was thinking too.

'This horse is fate's gift to you,' Sofi said at last. 'It's your kismet.'

'Yes,' Ahmet said, 'since it has come to my door and won't go away. But whose horse can it be?'

'There's a blazon on the saddle-cloth,' Sofi said. 'I seem to remember it. I've seen it somewhere very long ago. It must be the emblem of some powerful, formidable tribe. But whoever it belongs to, this horse is yours now. It has come to your door. It is a gift from the All-Wise.'

'From the All-Wise . . .' Ahmet murmured.

For good? Or for ill?

The cloud that passed over Ahmet's face did not escape Sofi's eye.

'This horse is yours now, whoever it belongs to,' he said again. 'But that emblem . . . It slips my memory. It's an old emblem, very old.'

13

Ahmet, resigned, accepts the horse as fate's gift

And there was this too, a horse so richly harnessed could not belong to just anybody.

'Don't think too much,' Sofi said. 'Take the horse and leave it on the road down yonder. If it comes to your door again, take it down again. Do this three times. And if you still find it at your door, it's yours. Be the owner Bey or Pasha, the Osmanli Sultan or the Shah of Persia, even the great Köroglu himself, you may give your head, but never this horse. Never.'

The sun was up now. The gilded clouds parted and a glittering vapour of light settled over the snow. Ahmet went to the horse. It was quite docile. He mounted it and rode down to the road. There he dismounted and returned on foot.

On reaching his house what should he see but the horse again, standing there beside Sofi! Three times he tried.

'I can't help it, uncle,' he said at last. 'It's God's will.'

One day the owner of this horse was sure to turn up. But Ahmet could never return it now. Rather than part with a gift from the All-Wise, a man would give up his own life . . .

He drew the horse into the stable with a mixture of elation and awe. He had never seen such a beautiful horse in all his life.

'If this horse's owner turns up to claim it in spite of our time-honoured tradition, there'll be trouble,' Sofi said with relish. 'Mount Ararat will give battle to the whole world when its anger is roused.'

'There'll be trouble,' Ahmet agreed.

It was soon known in the village that a pure-bred Arab horse had appeared out of the blue at Ahmet's door. Everyone came to look at it. The news was heard in the neighbouring villages and all through the land of Ararat. People flocked to see it and the horse's fame spread to Persia and beyond. Ahmet's unexpected windfall gave rise to much comment. Some thought it boded good and others ill . . .

Then from the lower plain, from Karakilise, the Black Church, from Gihadin, from Igdir came the Kurdish Beys. They saw the horse and envied Ahmet's luck.

For a long while there was no sign of the horse's owner.

Ahmet would mount his new-found steed, round up his friends and lead them on raids into Persian territory. They would seize sheep, horses and goods, and bring them back to Ararat.

But he was filled with misgivings. Surely the owner of this horse would come forward one day. Who could he be? A Bey perhaps, bloodthirsty, without mercy . . .

Six months went by. Ahmet forgot his fears and misgivings and even got used to the pleasure of mounting such a handsome steed.

Early one morning, as the sun, red and frozen, was resting on the flank of Mount Ararat, Sofi came to Ahmet. He leaned heavily on his stick and his long white beard trembled.

'Have you heard the news, Ahmet?' he asked.

'I have,' Ahmet said.

'It seems the Pasha of Beyazit, Mahmut Khan, is looking for a lost horse.'

'So I've heard,' Ahmet said.

'He's willing to give five horses to whoever brings it back to him, and fifty gold pieces too.'

'So I've heard,' Ahmet repeated.

'And he'll kill anyone in whose house the horse is found.'

16

'What can we do?' Ahmet said. 'This horse is my fate.'

'He'll come upon us with his armed men.'

'It's my fate.'

'He's a cruel Pasha, this Mahmut Khan.'

'It's my fate.'

'No one dares stand up against him.'

'This horse is a gift to me from the All-Wise.'

'Mahmut Khan does not know or care about customs and traditions. He's turned Ottoman.'

'I can't help that. The horse is still a sacred gift.'

Before a month had passed Mahmut Khan's men were at Ahmet's door.

'This is what the Pasha says,' they announced. 'Let him take any of my other horses, let him ask for cattle or money, anything. I'll give him anything he wishes in exchange for my horse.'

'Doesn't the Pasha know that this horse is a sacred gift to me?' Ahmet said. 'A horse that comes to you of its own accord is a gift of God and cannot be turned away. A man would rather die than part with it. Doesn't the Pasha know that?'

'The Pasha knows it very well, but still he wants his horse, because for him too the horse is precious; it's a gift from the Bey of Zilan, who is like a brother to him.'

But Ahmet would not be moved.

'Let the Pasha ask of me whatever he wishes,' he said. 'Let him ask for my services, my life, but not for the gift that has come to me from the All-Wise.'

'The Pasha says: "Let him not trust in his high mountain lair, nor in the couple of good-for-nothings who follow his lead. I can wipe them all off the face of the earth . . ." And he will,' they said.

Ahmet made no reply. Sofi was silent. At last, angry and frustrated, the Pasha's men left. And then the neighbours and people from nearby villages gathered around Ahmet. Even the valiant Kurdish Beys came to voice their support.

'Who's ever heard or seen such a thing!' they said. 'To give back a horse that comes from the All-Wise! Even though its owner be a Bey or a Pasha . . . Nobody's ever done such a thing.'

Ahmet did not speak much.

'I can't give it back,' was all he said.

The Pasha had never expected this. He went mad with rage. The tradition was one he knew very well and if a horse had come to his own castle in this way he would have died rather than give it back, whether it belonged to the Shah of Persia or to the Padishah of the Ottomans. But who was this Ahmet, this rustic nobody from the mountains to do this to him, the Pasha of Beyazit?

He had to get back his horse! In a moment the huge castle was in a ferment. He summoned his counsellors, his army officers, but no one could help him come to a decision. They knew only too well that he would have the whole of Ararat against him over this matter of the horse. Ahmet was not alone.

The Pasha summoned his friends the Kurdish Beys who were always ready to do his bidding. They came at once, mounted on handsome steeds, the Beys of Van and of Patnos, of Mount Süphan, of Mush and Bitlis. Mahmut Khan gave a great feast in their honour. He entertained them with a lavishness they had never encountered before. Then he held council with them and told them what was troubling him.

'A mere mountain man, a common raider, an unlicked whelp!' the Pasha repeated again and again. 'That such a one should steal my horse and insult me in this way!'

No one dared to mention the old tradition. No one dared tell him that all the people of Mount Ararat would give their lives before they allowed that horse to return to the castle. They said not a word, and their silence angered the Pasha.

'I want that horse back here,' he snapped, 'and you're to get it for me.'

Against their will the Kurdish Beys sent a messenger up to Ararat to speak with Ahmet.

Once again, Ahmet refused to give up the horse. And what's more, this was his message to them – words that were bitter as poison and as hard to swallow:

'Don't they know, those great Beys, that a man cannot reject a horse that comes to him as God's gift, a horse that has been turned away three times and has still returned to his door? Don't they know that this horse is a gift not to me but to all Ararat? They should know better than to ask us to give up a horse that is ours. But they are Beys no longer! They are the Pasha's slaves!'

The Kurdish Beys did not take offence at Ahmet's words. The people of Ararat are right, they said, but that won't do them any good. The Pasha will stop at nothing to have that horse.

And indeed when he saw that he would not achieve anything through the Kurdish Beys, Mahmut Khan acted at once. He summoned some soldiers and, accom-

The Kurdish Beys admit Ahmet's right to the Pasha's horse

panied by the Kurdish Beys, set out for Mount Ararat.

It was autumn. The foothills of Ararat are volcanic, and the rocks are red and purple. The loose stones and gravel slipped noisily under the horses' hooves like rushing water. One afternoon they reached Sorik, Ahmet's village. It was quite deserted, not a living soul was in sight. They stopped and gave the soldiers a rest there. Afterwards, the Pasha ordered the houses to be set on fire. It was then that a very old man emerged from one of the burning dwellings, his white head and beard dirty with soot. He was dressed in a brand-new blue-embroidered *shal-shapik*, the traditional Kurdish costume. It was old Sofi, and from under his thick overhanging eyebrows he looked accusingly at the Pasha. His eagle eyes flashed.

'All this for the sake of a horse?' he cried. 'Tell me, Pasha, tell me who, since the world began, who ever returned the horse that came to him of its own accord? Eh Pasha, tell me that! Ah, you must have turned Ottoman, Pasha. If not, would you ever have done this to us? Burnt our village, driven us out of our homes? The curse of Ararat be upon you! May the anger and fury of the mountain follow you wherever you go. I knew your father well. He was a valiant Bey. When you became a Pasha, you lost your sense of our old values. Your father would never have asked that a gift horse should be returned to him, never, not even if the horse had gone to stop at the door of a widow, a poor orphan, a thief, a pauper. But then, your father was a Bey and you've become a Pasha! The curse of Ararat be upon your head!'

The Pasha said nothing except: 'Tie up his hands, clap

an iron ring round his neck and throw him in the dungeon.'

There are many villages in the foothills of Mount Ararat and on its slopes. Mahmut Khan with the Kurdish Beys and his soldiers went from one village to another and found them all deserted. It was as though no man had ever set foot there.

The Pasha's anger knew no bounds.

'This is an insurrection!' he fumed as village after village turned out to be empty.

He was very tall, the Pasha, with an eagle nose, black eyes and a black curly beard. His whole demeanour, the way he waved his hand, the way he talked, expressed self-confidence. Always sparing of words, he was now more than usually thoughtful. He walked with long strides, an awe-inspiring figure. And all the time he was perspiring under his sable coat.

They swept along the plain of Igdir, on to Bashkoy, through the Ahuri Vale and up on to the Ahuri plateau. They met no one, not a shepherd, not a wayfarer, not a bandit. They saw no bird, no bear, no fox, no tiger, no living creature at all. The world was as void, as desolate as on the first day of creation.

'I'll find them,' the Pasha vowed. 'Even if the earth has opened and swallowed them up, I'll find them. Even if they've fled to Persia, to India, to China, to the ends of the earth.'

The Kurdish Beys were silent. They did not have the heart to say a word.

And now winter was upon them. The horses, the soldiers with their heavy packs were tired. They had scoured all the foothills of Great Ararat and had reached the foot of Little Ararat. The Pasha looked yellow and drawn and exhausted. Not to have met a single living creature on the way was what had infuriated him. He did not say a word to anyone. His followers did their best to guess his wishes by watching his face and gestures.

Yet still they kept searching the area round Ararat, though by now they had lost all hope.

One of the Kurdish Beys, Molla Kerim, braced himself to address Mahmut Khan.

'Pasha,' he said, 'the way things are going, we'll never find anyone, not if we search this huge mountain for a thousand years. These people know every nook and cranny and if they want to hide, the Devil himself won't find them. Strike me dead, Pasha, but it's the truth.'

The Pasha looked at him. There was infinite bitterness in his eyes, but he never said a word.

And so they went on combing the mountain. And the Pasha kept saying to himself: If I could only see one of these mountain people, just one beside that old Sofi, then I'd ask for nothing else.

In the end the Beys held a meeting between themselves. What was to be the end of this business? Where would all this running around lead them? And the Pasha refusing to listen to reason, getting angrier with every empty village they came to? No, they could not go on like this much longer, wandering about on the heights of Ararat. There would be a blizzard any day now. Or an avalanche that would wipe them all out. They had tried warning the Pasha of this, but he had not even heard them. After

23

*The Pasha's anger: 'Where have all those
mountain people vanished to?'*

discussing the matter at length, they agreed upon a proposition which they deemed acceptable to Mahmut Khan.

Molla Kerim was delegated to tell the Pasha of their deliberations. He stood deferentially before him, his hands joined as he spoke.

'Pasha,' he said, 'we have held a meeting of all the Beys, and have come to a decision. Give us three months, not four, and before winter is past, before you even begin to think of spring, we will find the horse and Ahmet too and bring them both to you.'

'It's not only Ahmet now, nor even the horse. Where have all these mountain people vanished to? That's what is driving me mad. To think we've seen no one but that old Sofi in all these mountain villages! No one, not a soul! I want those villagers too, all of them, before spring is here, before the snow melts.'

The Beys held another meeting and after long discussion Molla Kerim came again to the Pasha.

'We'll find those villagers too, Pasha,' he promised. 'They will be back by next spring.'

And so they made their way back to Beyazit, to the castle. The Pasha assembled all the Beys in his great Council chamber and rewarded every one of them with rich gifts. This pleased the Beys very much, but they were not a little worried. How would they set about finding Ahmet? Those mountain people could hide themselves till the crack of doom.

Mahmut Khan was an educated man, deeply attached to the Ottoman dynasty and proud of its fame and glory. His grandfather and great-grandfather had been mountain people up on Great Ararat. How they came to move down to the lowlands, or when, he did not know. All he knew was that his father, after having studied at the Moslem Seminary of Erzurum, had gone off to Istanbul and obtained a post at the court of the Ottoman Sultans. When he had come back it had been as a Pasha and by appointment of the Sultan. He was a powerful man, Mahmut Khan's father, an eagle of a man. It was he who had built a huge castle on the crags at Beyazit, and who had brought wise men and bards and poets to his court. He it was who had subdued the Kurdish Beys, every one of them, from Erzurum to Kars, from Kars to Van. He had lived a long and full life, his father, on horseback to the last. In the summer he moved up to the high pastures of Ararat, pitching his lofty pavilion on a spacious plateau just below the line where the glaciers began, and this pavilion was dearer to him than the imposing castle down below. The mountain people had respected his father, perhaps because they feared him . . . But his father too had a great respect for them and their customs. Mahmut Khan recalled how he would often summon the pipers to his pavilion, forty or fifty of them, and have them play all together in the old traditional manner.

If a horse of his father's had waited at the door of a man like Ahmet, would they have returned the horse to him? And if not, what would his father have done? The Pasha simply had no idea. He doubted whether the Beys would find the mountain folk. What if they had taken themselves off to faraway lands, to Iran or to Horasan? What if they had sought refuge in the mountain ranges of the Caucasus? How could the Beys reach them there?

Like his father, Mahmut Khan had studied in Erzurum first. Then he went to Istanbul where he served with distinction at the Sultan's court. He joined the Sultan's army and fought in many battles, earning himself a name for courage and daring. He travelled widely east and west. Damascus, Aleppo and Cairo were places he knew well, for he had lived there, and so were Sofia and Transylvania. Twelve years before his father's death he came back to Beyazit, to the castle, but only at his father's command. Otherwise, he would never have left Istanbul, for he liked that city above all others. At his father's death he became Pasha in his stead.

At first he found it difficult to get used to these uncouth people, to these stern mountains. The castle had no equal even in Istanbul, but that was not enough to fill his life. Then he noticed the beauty of the women. Nowhere in the world could a man come across such graceful creatures. First he married an Armenian girl. Then he took the daughter of a Kurdish Bey. His third wife came from the Caucasus and his fourth from the shores of Lake Urmiyé, in Iran. Three daughters and seven sons were born to him. Mahmut Khan himself had five brothers, but they and all the rest of his tribe had gone down to settle on the plain of Igdir and he had very few ties with them now.

His one great passion was deer-hunting. Each spring he would set out with a group of his best marksmen and go hunting up in the mountains of Esrük and Süphan, near

27

Lake Van, and in the steep valleys of Sor and Zilan. He would return with hundreds of deerskins.

The Pasha's three daughters all had names that began with Gül, which means rose. One was called Gülistan, the other Gülriz and the third Gülbahar. Gülistan, whose mother was the Pasha's Armenian wife, was tall and slender with red hair and huge hazel eyes. She followed the fashions of the Imperial Court and had all her clothes made in Istanbul. Fair-haired Gülriz also dressed after the Istanbul fashion. She had a long swan-like neck and very blue eyes framed by curling lashes. She was the bookish one among the three sisters. Even as a child she had memorized all of Ahmedi Hani's poetry, and her father, whose favourite she was, would often summon her to recite poetry at his court.

Gülbahar was not like her sisters. Of medium height with a full figure and a clear bright complexion, the colour of burnt straw, she always dressed in the many-skirted costume of the mountain women. Again like the mountain women she combed her hair into forty little plaits. She wore anklets of gold and pearl and emerald, and a gold necklace. She was clever, Gülbahar, saying little, always with that half-smile on her lips. The Pasha's children hardly ever set foot outside the castle, nor did they mix with the people of the town or countryside. But Gülbahar was not like them. She liked to see people. She took part in all the gatherings and never missed a wedding or a festival.

The people of Beyazit town and the villagers of Ararat Mountain loved her and looked upon her as a saint. Wherever someone was needed to nurse the sick or care for the old, Gülbahar was always on hand to ride out there, more expert in the saddle than the most seasoned rider. The Pasha never interfered in her activities. He contented himself with keeping an eye on her, and often he would think to himself: 'Ah, if that girl had been a boy, she could easily have held sway over the whole of Ararat.'

Gülbahar hated life at the castle. She did not get on well with her sisters either. She was already twenty-one years old and her warm sad eyes burned with a faraway yearning. The village people never called her by her name. For them she was the 'Smiling Maid'.

At the castle, it was Gülbahar who was the most interested in the story of her father's horse. Something must have made this horse go to Ahmet's house, she was sure. So she sought out old Sofi in the castle dungeon and asked him to tell her the whole story. Gülbahar loved the old man, and so she came back the next day and every day after that. She brought him food from the Pasha's kitchens and plied him with questions about the horse.

'I can swear to it, child, it's God's truth,' Sofi said to her again and again. 'Three times the horse was left on the road far below. I took it down myself. And three times it came again to stand at Ahmet's door. That horse is a gift to Ahmet from the All-Wise. He can never give it back, never. The whole of Ararat would die rather than let him do such a thing!'

One day Sofi asked Gülbahar to bring him a pipe. She complied at once and found him a very old one, seasoned by maybe a hundred years of use. But she was surprised and doubtful. How could Sofi play on the pipe at his age? Playing the pipe required good teeth and strong breath. It was not a job for the old. And then she suddenly saw that this bent aged man's teeth were as white and perfect as her own.

Gülbahar, the Pasha's daughter, fascinated, as old Sofi plays on the pipe

Eagerly Sofi seized the pipe and as soon as he started playing Gülbahar was carried away. Never before had she heard anything like this. She sat down on the threshold of the dungeon and leaned against the wall while Sofi played and played, like one possessed, tirelessly, ceaselessly.

When the piping stopped Gülbahar awoke as though rousing herself out of a long sleep.

'Sofi, who made up that tune?' she asked, in a faint voice.

'Our forefathers,' answered Sofi. 'Once upon a time the mountain shook in anger and then our fathers made this tune that tells of its wrath.'

Gülbahar would come back each day before sunrise and stand at the door of the dungeon, and each day Sofi would play to her the tune of Ararat's wrath. But however much she plied him with questions, he would not tell her what it was that had caused the mountain to burst into mighty anger.

'Something made the mountain very angry,' was all Sofi would say. 'And then our forefathers made up this ballad, but I know only the tune I play on the pipe. It's the bards who can tell you the words. I'm a piper, not a bard.'

It was in vain that Gülbahar pleaded with him. Sofi would not recite the words of the song.

'Gentle lady, doesn't my pipe tell you of itself the story of the mountain's wrath? If it doesn't, then alas! it means I'm too old to play the pipe any more.'

Gülbahar had often heard this famous old ballad before, sung by the people of the mountain and also by skilled bards and minstrels. But somehow, when Sofi played it, it was different. Who knows, if he told it, how he would tell it . . .

Old Sofi in the dungeon of Beyazit Castle

The Pasha knew that his daughter had taken an interest in old Sofi, that she took him food in the dungeon and sat there for hours to listen to his piping.

One day he had Sofi brought up into his presence.

'Sofi,' the Pasha said, 'I cannot set you free unless I have the horse. Unless I have Ahmet. You shall be free if you promise to bring me back the horse and Ahmet too.'

Sofi glared at him defiantly.

'That can never be, Pasha,' he said. 'That horse came to Ahmet as a sacred gift from the All-Wise. Even if he wanted to he could not part with it. And I would never deliver Ahmet into your hands, Pasha.'

Angrier than ever, Mahmut Khan sent Sofi down into the dungeon again and then called for his daughter.

'Gülbahar,' he said, 'you will have nothing more to do with that old man.'

In the castle the Pasha's every word was law.

Not many days afterwards a messenger arrived bearing news from the Bey of the Hayderan tribe. 'Let the Pasha's mind be at ease. We have found out where Ahmet has fled with the horse and the mountain people. Soon he and the horse will be in your hands.'

And indeed it was so. Ahmet, having roused all the mountain people, had led them down far south into the Hakkari Mountains to stay with the Shemdinan Kurds.

So the Beys took counsel together and finally entrusted the son of the Bey of Milan with the task of going to the Shemdinan Kurds. Musa Bey found Ahmet in his mauve-embroidered tent among hundreds of other tents in a broad valley, high up in the mountains.

Ahmet welcomed him warmly and Musa Bey told him why he had come.

'The Pasha wants to see you,' he said. 'He wants nothing else of you, not even the horse. He wants the mountain people to return to their homes too. The Beys have talked him into forgiving you, and now the Pasha is curious. He wants to know you. That's what he told the Beys. He must be a valiant man, this Ahmet, he said. Only let me see him and I'll make him a present of a dozen horses. The Beys sent me to you to tell you all this.'

The Beys of Shemdinan and the leaders of the Ararat people held long meetings to discuss the matter. Some were of the opinion that the invitation was a trap. Others did not agree. How could so many exalted Beys stoop to such a stratagem? And Mahmut Khan? A prestigious Ottoman Pasha? Would they all stoop to such an action for the sake of a horse? The Pasha was simply curious to know what kind of a man his horse had chosen to run away to. It could be nothing else.

From Musa Bey Ahmet heard for the first time that Sofi was in the castle dungeon. He was dismayed. When they had fled from their homes on Mount Ararat Ahmet had pleaded with Sofi to come too, but in vain. The old man had clung to the mountain as firmly as one of its great rugged rocks. How could he have imagined that the Pasha would take him prisoner!

'Sofi's all right, don't worry,' Musa Bey said. And he told him about Gülbahar, the Pasha's daughter, and how she had befriended the old man in his prison.

Ahmet felt a little easier.

'Musa Bey,' he said, 'since you have come to me in

friendship, how can I turn you away? I'll go back to Ararat and see the Pasha. The tribe will return with me. Only one thing I cannot do. The Pasha shall not see his horse again.'

'The Pasha only asked to see you,' Musa Bey said again. 'He wants nothing else.'

And so one day in spring the mountain people trooped back to Ararat.

All the Kurdish Beys were there to meet Ahmet, and he was taken into the presence of the Pasha.

Mahmut Khan showed not a trace of anger. He greeted Ahmet haughtily and with a touch of scorn.

'Well, here you are then, Sultan of Ararat!' he said. 'And where's my horse?'

'The horse is with me,' was Ahmet's reply.

'You stole it,' the Pasha said and laughed. 'Do you know how I punish those who steal from me?'

Ahmet did not flinch.

'I never stole any horse of yours, Pasha,' he retorted. 'That horse came to me as a gift from the All-Wise. It can never be yours again. Your ancestors were mountain people like us. Don't you know the old custom?'

The blood rushed to the Pasha's head.

'No, I don't,' he shouted. 'Either I have my horse or I'll have your head. Throw him into the dungeon.'

The Beys who had brought Ahmet to the castle were struck dumb.

'Pasha, Pasha!' Ahmet cried. 'You will have my head then, for you'll never see that horse again, not in this castle!'

Musa Bey had never dreamed such a thing could happen.

'But Pasha,' he protested, 'how can you do this? It's not

35

just. I went and brought Ahmet to you, but not for this, not so that you should take him prisoner! You deceived me. You lied to me.'

Mahmut Khan saw red.

'Throw this man into the dungeon too,' he thundered.

And so Musa Bey too was imprisoned.

Then Mahmut Khan spoke to the Kurdish Beys:

'Is this how you keep your word? You promised to bring the horse together with Ahmet. Where is it? I want that horse. I will not have such an insult cast at me, at my family. I will not have it said that the Pasha could not get his horse back from a mere mountain peasant.'

'It's not going to be easy, Pasha,' the Beys said, 'but we will bring the horse back to you.'

The story of the horse and of the fortunes of Ahmet and Sofi and Musa Bey soon spread far and wide. From Van to Malatya, from Malatya to the Caucasus, all over Anatolia, wandering bards and minstrels began to sing songs and ballads telling of the adventures of Ahmet and the horse.

And now the Pasha had against him not only the mountain people, but also the whole tribe of Milan, whose chief was Musa Bey's father. Nobody could forgive the Pasha for setting Ahmet such an ignoble trap.

Down in the castle dungeon Musa Bey had made his peace with Ahmet.

'I suspected nothing,' he said, 'or I'd never have brought you here. Forgive me. And now they'll have to kill me first before they do anything else to you . . .'

Old Sofi could not help it. He was overjoyed to see Ahmet. He embraced and hugged him again and again. Then he produced his pipe and began to play. He played the ballad of Ararat's wrath and tears came to the eyes of Ahmet and Musa Bey as they listened to him. Suddenly Sofi stopped and handed the pipe over to Ahmet. Ahmet was sick at heart.

'The curse of Ararat be upon the Pasha's head and upon those Beys too,' he said, and he put the pipe to his mouth.

The sound was different, as though it were quite another pipe. The tune was the same that Sofi had been playing, the wrath of Ararat, but Ahmet's piping had a quality at once melting and rousing, that seemed to bring to life the stones and all the inanimate things of the mountain.

From within the castle Gülbahar heard the strains of the pipe and wondered at the new sound. She was afraid of disobeying her father's orders, yet still she found herself drawn down to the dungeon.

And so she saw Ahmet for the first time and a new feeling of warmth and tenderness came over her. She sat down at the foot of the prison wall and listened to Ahmet's piping, oblivious to the whole world.

Her sense of outrage at her father's behaviour grew stronger. She felt she must do something to make up for his cruelty to these brave honourable men.

She hurried to the kitchens and with her handmaidens prepared the daintiest dishes she knew. Then she told her menservants to take them to the prisoners.

Her mother got wind of what she was up to.

'If the Pasha hears about this,' she said appalled, 'he'll have you beheaded, and me too.'

'What matter what the Pasha does?' Gülbahar retorted. 'After dishonouring himself in such a way . . .'

The days passed without bringing news of the horse. Not a word came from the Kurdish Beys. And so Musa Bey and Ahmet continued to lie in the castle dungeon, and all the while Gülbahar sent them food and delicacies, but very secretly. Sometimes she would go to the dungeon and watch them from a distance.

In the end she could not help herself.

'Sofi,' she whispered to the old man, 'I must talk to Ahmet. I'll come one night. Tell him.'

Ahmet's long curly beard, golden yellow, flowed down in sheeny waves. His eyelashes cast a shadow of sad yearning over his large clear blue eyes. Ahmet was tall. His long narrow face had the poignant expression of a wounded roe-deer. It was as though the sorrow and longing and passion of all humankind was concentrated in this face. She saw it in a dream, in an enchantment, floating behind a luminous haze. His eyes, his gestures, had a quality that warmed your heart and carried you away into the glow of another world, far and unknown. It seemed to Gülbahar that she had always known Ahmet, almost as though they had been born at the same time and had grown up together, so familiar, so close to her he was . . . Perhaps at some wedding or festival? Up in the pastures? At a hunt? . . . Perhaps . . . Who knows? Perhaps in her dreams . . . So close, so intimate . . .

'But how can you, my dear?' Sofi said. 'The keeper of the dungeon will never agree. He'll tell the Pasha and the Pasha will have us all beheaded.'

But a worm was eating her. It gave her no rest. At night sleep would not come, and as she lay awake Ahmet's face passed before her eyes. It came and went and came again like a bright beam of light, smiling, yet with a look of anguish in the large blue eyes. Some old incurable wound, some great sorrow Ahmet must have, locked deep within him. Perhaps he had no one in this world, no mother or father, no brother or sisters, no loved ones at all . . . Kithless, forlorn . . . The thought hurt her like a poison flowing into her breast. I must talk to him, she said to herself. I must help him, and soothe him, and relieve his loneliness.

Why could she think only of him and nothing else? Why was he before her eyes all the time? Even in her sleep, even in her dreams . . . Wherever she looked she saw nothing but his image. Whatever she touched it was him. Whichever way she went her feet dragged her back towards the dungeon. She knew it well now, this dungeon. It had a massive iron door with a heavy lock and chain. The arch over the door and the walls on each side were of rough limestone unevenly set.

The keeper of the dungeon was Memo. The Pasha trusted him implicitly and loved him as much as his own children. Memo's father had been one of his most faithful retainers, a brave soldier too. But he had been killed in a battle when Memo was only two years old.

Memo was young and brave. He did not know the meaning of fear and was ready to give his life for the Pasha. Men like him were ideal jailers. He kept to himself and talked very little. Gülbahar could not remember a single time when Memo had looked at her face or into her eyes. Whenever they met he blushed and turned pale by turns and his hands trembled. Gülbahar had decided once and for all that Memo had a bashful nature. She had

39

Memo, the keeper of the dungeon

never seen him otherwise than with downcast eyes, tongue-tied and blushing like a girl.

Gülbahar continued to have food prepared in the castle kitchens and sent down to the prisoners. For Memo she would take special care, bringing the food to him herself.

'I've cooked this with my own hands, brother Memo,' she would tell him. 'Just for you . . .'

And so the days went by. A few times Gülbahar managed to catch a glimpse of Ahmet, and she owed this to Memo. He would disappear suddenly and Gülbahar would find he had left the door of the dungeon unlocked. She would stand on the stone staircase and talk to Sofi, but all the while her eyes would be on the pit of the dungeon where Ahmet was slowly pacing up and down.

High up in the walls of the dungeon were a few long, narrow slits through which shafts of daylight pierced the darkness. The dungeon had been built on the edge of a precipice overlooking the plain of Beyazit where the long, long caravan road stretched towards the horizon.

From time to time the jingle of bells from a passing caravan would raise echoes in the pit of the dungeon. All sounds coming from the mountain or rising from the plain would echo and re-echo in this dungeon. In the pit there was just one loophole, large as a hand and set at the height of a man. This loophole was renowned throughout the countryside. All the people hereabouts blessed the master-builder because he had left this opening. They venerated him as a saint. He had been an Assyrian Christian, who it was said had spent long years in prison and knew better than anyone the misery and burden of a dark dungeon. Whatever happens, he was reported to have vowed, I'll leave a loophole in this dungeon. Whatever it may cost me, a light will pierce the darkness of a dungeon for the first time in the world, and it'll be the dungeon I have built. No tyrant will ever be able to seal off these loopholes nor put out the sources of light that I have contrived.

When the castle was built and finished the masterbuilder disappeared without a trace. He left a letter for the Pasha. 'Whoever attempts to close up the loopholes I have made,' the letter read, 'will be pulling down the very foundations of this castle. For I have built this castle upon the light of these loopholes. Whoever destroys the sources of these lights will be cursed for eternity and all his descendants after him. Whoever does not make known this letter to all the occupants of this castle, now and to come, his race too will dry up and wither.'

So it came to pass that since that day no one dared do anything about these sources of light and for that reason Beyazit Castle was a legend in the minds of men. Whoever came to be cast into its dungeon heaped blessings on the memory of the Assyrian, Süleyman the Builder.

Summer or winter, when the prisoner looked out through the narrow loophole, the world he saw was an unfamiliar world. It all seemed to float before him: the tracks that ran across the plain towards the horizon, the snows, the passing caravans, the cranes and bustards, the wild geese and ducks, and the constellations of stars that studded the sky above the low hills. Against a background of twinkling stars and tracks and valleys, each with its ribbon of water, winding towards the horizon, the plain seemed to float in three bands, separated by broad streaks of misty radiance. On being set free the prisoner would seek for days that plain he had looked at for so long through the loophole of the dungeon, that world that changed from one moment to the next, that different, enchanted world, now wrapped in an orange glow, now yellow and sun-drenched, sometimes blue, sometimes violet or green, of burnished copper, smothered in light, bright with flowers, covered with snow . . . But in vain. He never found it again, as though that plain, that whole world, had been spirited away the minute he came out of the dungeon.

Sofi, Ahmet and Musa Bey would take turns to look through the loophole as the spring mellowed into summer over the plain. In the morning, a faint, hardly visible mist would rise from the ground and the hills would be hidden by a veil of blue. Gradually the mist would turn pink, and then disperse.

And now Gülbahar was burning with love from head to foot. Love penetrated to the marrow of her bones. Whatever she touched, every object, every living thing, flared up with the fire of her love. She could not keep still for a moment. All through the castle she roamed, in a whirlwind of love. One moment she was in ecstasy and the next plunged in darkest despair. A sudden fear, as violent as her love, would overwhelm her. It is only for a moment, she said to herself, for as long as his stay in prison lasts . . . It was all she would ever see of Ahmet her whole life long. Never could it be otherwise, never. Not even if the Shah and the Padishah willed it would she ever see Ahmet again. Not even if the great Sheikh of the Caravans himself willed it. Everything else could happen in this world, but when Ahmet left this prison Gülbahar would never see him again, not even once, not even from far far away.

A torrent of love and despair, death, separation, tyranny overwhelmed her.

Then one day her fever died down. She was tired. Her whole body ached as though it had been beaten in a mortar. She swayed on her feet. Nobody knew what to make of this sudden change. The Gülbahar storm was over.

For three days she crept about the castle in a trance, silent, stiff, like a corpse risen from the grave. Her face was dull and yellow. Her hair had lost its lustrous sheen, her teeth their whiteness. Only her eyes shone, huge, glittering . . . The pretty dimples in her cheeks were fixed in a smile, her whole body was rigid, in the grip of some deep emotion.

And then one evening a change came over her. The storm of love burst out again. Love and joy flowed from her, casting a radiance over the ground, the very stones she stepped on. She could hardly wait for the night to fall. Running out of the castle, she stood for a while watching the smithy from a distance. A shower of sparks came from the doorway, hiding the figure of Hüso the smith. She walked on to the tomb of the poet Ahmedi Hani,* where she knelt in worship and prayed and invoked his aid. Gülbahar's prayers, like everything about her, were like a torrent, a torrent that could not be dammed. As she came away from the tomb the longed-for night was darkening the slopes of Ararat. It was raining in a thin drizzle.

She could see everything now, down to the smallest detail. There was no escape for her. She would go straight on to meet her fate, whatever happened, at whatever cost.

*Ahmedi Hani: famous Kurdish scholar and poet who lived in Beyazit town in the sixteenth century and whose tomb is near the castle.

In her room was a heavy chest of carved walnut wood. She took out her Caucasian necklace of ruby and gold, a gift from her grandmother. She took out her ring, her pearl bracelets, the gold anklets and the nose-ring her uncle had brought her from his travels in India and Afghanistan. She put all the jewels she possessed into a velvet pouch and made straight for the dungeon.

Memo was in his room close by the dungeon. She knocked and he opened the door. A long sword hung over his right hip down to his ankles. He wore an *aba* made from the skin of a chestnut colt and embroidered with gold and silver thread. On his head was the long peaked felt *külah* of the region.

An ineffable joy suffused Memo's face at the sight of Gülbahar, a strange bliss . . . It did not escape her, although it was gone in an instant to be replaced by an expression of despair so black and violent that she began to lose heart. Memo blushed and looked down. She saw that his lips and hands were trembling, and suddenly she held out the velvet pouch.

'Take these, Memo,' she said. 'I give them all to you.'

Memo took the pouch and stared. His hands shook more than ever, like fluttering birds.

'You will let me see Ahmet who is in the dungeon . . .'

The pouch fell from Memo's hands on to the stone floor with a ringing clatter. Gülbahar bent down, picked it up and held it out to Memo again. He did not take it. There was not a drop of blood in his face. It was like parchment.

'Take these jewels, Memo. Take them, but let me see that man inside. You can go afterwards to my father and tell him all. Tell him so that he may strike off my head.'

45

Memo remained motionless for a while. Then very slowly he lifted his head and looked at her. There was agony in his eyes, the last gleam of life in the eyes of a dying man. She could not bear it. She lowered her eyes in her turn.

His hand went slowly and heavily to his waist, and pulled out the key to the dungeon. He thrust it at Gülbahar and turned away.

She stood there dazed, not knowing whether to weep or rejoice. Suddenly she burst into tears. She sank down at the door of Memo's room and wept her heart out. Oh, how she wanted to leave the key there and turn away, but she couldn't. She forced herself to her feet and with faltering steps, her heart pounding at her breast, she approached the door of the dungeon. Inserting the heavy key into the lock, she opened the door. The inside of the dungeon was pitch-black. From the depths below a light glimmered very faintly. Gülbahar began to grope her way down the ancient stone steps that had been hewn into the rock hundreds of years before the castle ever existed. No sign of life was visible. It was as though some dense dregs had settled in those depths, forming a smooth glinting surface. There were no dank odours in this dungeon, only a sour smell of tanned skin and hide rose to Gülbahar's nostrils.

At the bottom of the steps she stopped and peered into the darkness.

'Sofi!' she called out softly. 'Sofi . . .'

Sofi, all dishevelled, came hurrying to the steps.

'My lady!' he cried in alarm. 'How did you get here? The Pasha will have us all beheaded. Go away, quickly. You're the first woman ever to enter this dungeon since it was built. Quick, quick, go . . . Does anyone know you're here?'

'Where is Ahmet? Tell him.'

There was nothing Sofi could do.

'All right,' he said and turned away.

From the thick black depths of the dungeon came the sound of whispering. Then all was plunged in a deep silence. Gülbahar's heart was drumming loudly. It seemed to her she heard it echoing against the cold stones of the dungeon.

She waited impatiently, her eagerness increasing, her heart fluttering now like a wounded bird's. And then she saw the tall shadow moving out of the darkness and she felt suddenly limp and faint. Her head whirled and she leaned against the wall.

At the feel of Ahmet's breath on her face she came to herself. Yet still they stood there, silent, motionless.

At last Ahmet spoke.

'Gülbahar!' he said. 'It's you . . .'

'Yes . . .' she whispered.

It was as though they had been friends, sweethearts, lovers since time out of mind. A cloud of love fell over them, warm and fair and friendly, and spread through the whole dungeon.

Into this dark place Sofi had somehow managed to lure a group of red-legged partridges, and these partridges would break into song at all hours of the night or the day. And now, suddenly, from the dregs of darkness there rose the twittering of a partridge. Gülbahar started at this unexpected sound and put out her hand. Ahmet took it and led her up the steps, to the watchtower which topped the dungeon. A couple of paces in front of them was a deep

47

The meeting of Ahmet and Gülbahar

chasm. Over the plain and the hills, dim under the star-light, there fell a great darkness, the shadow of Mount Ararat. A moon was hanging above the mountain, dull and lustreless, one side dimmed and worn. After a while a black cloud came and hid it from view. Gülbahar still held Ahmet's hand in a burning grasp.

They sat there in a corner of the watchtower until the first cocks crew in the night. Then, like the bursting of a flame, their hands fell apart. Gülbahar did not want to go yet. She wanted it to last a little more, till daybreak, this marvellous feeling of Ahmet's hand in hers. Who cared what happened! Who cared if after this her blood was shed over this earth! She clasped his hand once again. It was like two flames joining together.

The night was growing steadily paler. Their locked hands dragged apart again and Ahmet rose and walked away. She heard the heavy dungeon door closing upon him.

For a long while Gülbahar remained there, not know-ing what to do, where to go, utterly exhausted. Then her eyes fell on the big dungeon key. She went to Memo's room. The door was wide open and Memo was not there. Suddenly frightened, she started looking for him all through the castle grounds. Finally she came upon him sitting beside the great gate of the inner wall. He was still as a corpse and did not look up at the sound of her foot-steps.

She waited, then dropped the key on to his lap.

'Thank you, Memo, brother,' she said. 'I'll never forget your goodness to me.'

He never stirred or gave a sign that he had heard her.

The sun was rising. Gülbahar turned and went into the castle.

Down in the darkness of the dungeon Ahmet felt as desolate as a stone now. He could not believe it had happened, this miracle. Gülbahar's warm spell, the pungent odour of her body could not be real. He must have had a dream last night. He tried to shake off his doubts and love and happiness filled him to the brim. For a moment only. The feeling of emptiness, of unreality, of desolation soon took hold of him again.

So this was why the horse had come to him. It was the design of the Almighty. Gülbahar, like the horse, was a gift to him from the Almighty. He must be worthy of her, this girl who was like the flowers of Ararat, pungent, crisp, lovely. His head whirled.

'Sofi,' he said, 'give me the pipe.'

That day Gülbahar could not be still. She drifted aimlessly through the castle, without eating, absent, like a sleep-walker.

Her father would never set Ahmet free. And even if he did, would he allow his daughter to be joined to him? Would a Pasha ever give his daughter to a mountain peasant? And a rebel too?

The sound of the pipe roused her to life, and her whole body quivered.

If only Ahmet could escape . . . If he could come one night and swing her up on the back of his horse . . . They would ride off into the desert below where the deer roamed at large, where the Kurdish nomad tribes pitched their high tents, always open and hospitable. Also, down in the plain the mountain people were looked upon as different creatures, as though from another world, almost sacred.

But what was the use? Her father would ferret them out wherever they fled. The Ottoman Empire was powerful. Its arm stretched to the ends of the earth. They would kill Ahmet, ah they would kill him! Her heart burned at the very thought.

She must see him while she could. Tonight again . . . Every night . . . But what if her father heard of it? He would kill them all. And there was something strange about Memo too. To have refused all those precious jewels! And then to hand the key over to her just like that, without a word. She did not want to think of him. The memory of the wounded look in his eyes disturbed her too much. She did her best to banish his image from her mind. Deep down she had always known there was something about Memo . . . Something . . . He had always acted oddly towards her. Gülbahar had known only too well, when she had gone to him for the key, that he would do anything for her, whatever it cost him.

Yes, she must see Ahmet tonight, every night for as long as he stayed a prisoner in this dungeon. But how could she go to Memo for the key again and look upon his suffering face, without flinching, knowing all this was torture worse than death to him?

A feeling of defiance was growing in her, a revolt against her father, the castle, the traditions, against Mount Ararat and the whole world.

From the palace came her father's voice, deep and strong. Mahmut Khan was a handsome man. He had always seemed to Gülbahar like a mighty eagle. She loved him more than anyone in the world and admired

51

him too. Mahmut Khan knew that his daughter thought the world of him.

Evening came, the sun set and Gülbahar still roamed through the castle with no apparent aim. Yet her steps were taking her back more and more insistently to her father's apartments. The sound of voices had died out now. Everyone had retired. Her father must be preparing himself for the evening *namaz* prayers.

Suppose I were to go to him, she thought . . . Suppose I were to fall on my knees and entreat him . . . I am not your daughter, I am just a suppliant come to your House, Mahmut Khan. Dragging myself on my knees I come . . . Spare Ahmet for me, let him go. Don't deny your noble race, Mahmut Khan. You come from the glorious mountain of Ararat too. My grandfather would always tell of those days, did you never hear him, Mahmut Khan? We used to live where the mighty eagles had their eyries.

A soldier opened the door of the Pasha's apartments. At that moment she almost went in, determined to throw herself at his feet. With an effort she held herself back. Her heart leaped to her mouth as she crept away. If it were just for herself it would be easy. But when the Pasha learnt of Ahmet, he was sure to have him put to death.

It was midnight and still she could not sleep. The stillness was complete save for an occasional jangling of chains rising from the dungeon. The whole of Beyazit town was plunged in deep slumber. Gülbahar tossed and turned in her bed.

It could never be. She would be found out in the end and, oh, they would kill Ahmet . . . Nothing was a secret for long in this castle. Her sisters had already noticed a change in her . . . And Memo, the keeper of the dungeon, wouldn't he give them away in the end? Out of fear, to save his own skin? Memo? . . . Give her away?

All these thoughts and fears gave her no rest. She rose from her bed and before she knew it she was at the dungeon door. She paused, then went on to Memo's room. But somehow she could not bring herself to knock. For a long time she stood there, a prey to conflicting feelings, fear, shame, pain, undefined vague sensations . . . Sudsenly the door opened. Memo had sensed her presence outside. She looked at him and turned away impulsively, but he sprang after her and held out the key.

'You can talk in here,' he said in a faint strangled voice, and pointed to his room.

With all her strength Gülbahar forced open the iron door of the dungeon and hurried down the stone steps.

'Sofi,' she called. 'Sofi . . .'

Ahmet had been waiting since nightfall, scarcely daring to breathe, starting up at the slightest sound. He ran to her at once and their hands met like two burning flames.

Why had Memo pointed to his room and told her to talk with Ahmet there? Was he a saint, this Memo? Could there really be a human being so selflessly devoted? She felt strangely crushed. Quickly, she pulled Ahmet away, up to the roof of the dungeon. There, outside the watchtower on the edge of the precipice facing the east, they sank down against the wall and sat quite still, hand in hand, heart to heart. In the silence of the night they could hear the blood coursing in each other's veins.

Then she spoke and her voice was like a lament.

'Is it true what they are saying?' she asked.

'What have you heard?' Ahmet queried.

'That if you do not give up that horse within forty days,

53

my father will have you beheaded, all three of you, Sofi and Musa Bey too . . .'

'It's true,' he said.

She murmured something in a moan, but he could not make out what.

'Gülbahar, do you remember me?' Ahmet asked. 'Up in the summer pastures above Lake Küp, at the wedding festivities?'

'You have haunted my mind ever since that day,' she said. 'You were the one who led the dance. And you, you remember me then?'

'As clearly as I see you now. You were wearing red coral anklets.'

Gülbahar was floating in a pleasant dream.

'Up on the summer pastures that year, higher up even than Lake Küp,' she said. 'I remember the bard with the long long hair who sang the epic of Siy Ahmedé Silivi. Three days and three nights he sang and still it wasn't finished! They said it was only the beginning of the poem.'

'It's a very very long poem,' Ahmet said. 'I've heard that bard recite the whole of it. Forty days it took him to get to the end.'

Suddenly Gülbahar drew a sigh like a sob.

'He'll have you executed, the three of you. Aaah . . .'

'How can he do this to Sofi who's at least a hundred years old?' Ahmet wondered. 'He can put us to death, but Sofi! That's cruel. I've never heard of anything so cruel, never. Poor Sofi! And he so old . . . But he doesn't seem to care, Gülbahar. He's so cheerful down in that dungeon, playing on the pipe, laughing . . . I can't bear the idea of Sofi being beheaded, I can't. I wish I could

54

think of a way to save him. One doesn't put to death a man who is so old. Do you know that the Pasha has sent word down to us that Sofi will be the first to go under the axe, before our very eyes?'

'None of you must die, not one,' she said, and suddenly she put her arms around him.

'If the Pasha learns of this he'll have you executed too, with us . . .'

'If it comes to that, then let him!' she countered and her voice rang with defiance. 'Who'll care then?'

Ahmet was silent. Then he said: 'My heart grieves for Musa Bey. All because of me . . . Sometimes I wonder whether I ought to give up that horse and save his life and Sofi's too. But the tribesmen would never agree. And even if they did, how could I ever face them again? They'd despise me. They'd say, "He feared for his life and gave back to the Pasha the horse that came to him as a gift from the All-Wise." But Musa Bey? Must he die? And Sofi? Ah Sofi . . .'

There was a lump in her throat strangling her. She rested her head on his shoulder and the tears ran down her cheeks.

'Oh curse that horse,' she thought. 'Curse it, curse it . . .'

It was cockcrow already. Soon the sun came up over the shoulder of Ararat, blood-red, not the sun at all but a glass apple, a crystal-red apple, large and round and shining.

Like a flame splitting in two their hands tore apart. Ahmet went down into the dungeon. Gülbahar did not move. She sat gazing after him. All the strength was drained from her body. It was mid-morning when she rose, like a drowning woman.

55

If the Pasha said something he meant it. Nothing could save them now, not even a decree from the Sultan himself. Mahmut Khan had never been known to go back on his decisions.

There was no hope for Gülbahar, not a glimmer of hope. Like a heavy flood of rising water despair engulfed her on all sides. Forty days of happiness to last her a whole life long . . . That was all that fortune would give her. Forty days of happiness . . . And that was the happiness of holding the hand of a man who was going to die, of embracing a dead man . . . Even if Ahmet returned the horse, even if he were not beheaded and got away safe and sound, Gülbahar would never see him again, never. He would go back to his mountain home and she would be left behind, here in this castle, solitary as the stone at the bottom of the well. Life would be over for her, one way or another.

Ah, but Ahmet would never consent to return the horse. Before Gülbahar's very eyes they would strike his head off. Then they would stick the gory head on to a pole and parade it all through the town. His golden hair and beard would be smeared with blood. The words of the old lament rose to her lips: They have smeared it all in crimson blood, that dear dear face I feared to kiss . . . And she could not hold back her tears.

His body would be cast down from the battlements. Ahmet's dear body smashing to pieces against the rocks, crashing down to the bottom of the precipice.

'That dear dear face I feared to kiss . . .' The lament

56

grew in her, gave her the strength to think of ways and means to save Ahmet.

'I want him to live,' she said, gritting her teeth. 'Even if I am never to see him again, even if I have to see him marry another up in his mountain home, even if I have to die for him to live.'

Surely there was some hope yet. Would Musa Bey's father do nothing to save his son? And what about the other Kurdish Beys of whose lies Musa Bey was the innocent victim? . . . The least they could do was to go and plead with the mountain people and say: Give us the horse, people of Ararat, to save three human lives . . . Would the mountain people refuse? Stern and uncompromising they might be, but they would not easily turn away someone who came to them as a suppliant. Tradition was everything with them, and to refuse would be against all tradition. Gülbahar began to gain hope.

And then an idea flashed through her mind. Why not go myself? she thought. The mountain people will never never deny a woman supplicant. If the Beys won't go, if they fear my father, then I will. I'll go to the mountain people. I'll save my Ahmet's life. And I'll never see him again, not once, till I die. He will marry another and have many many children . . .

She must talk to someone, someone she could trust. Should she go at once to the mountain people? Or send a message to Musa Bey's father?

All day long she hesitated. There was Yusuf, her own brother, of the same mother . . . Yusuf was very much attached to her, but could she trust him? Would he agree to come with her if she went to ask for the horse? There was also the risk that the mountain people might hold him

Gülbahar goes to her brother Yusuf and tells him all

as hostage in exchange for Ahmet. They might do the same with her if she went alone . . . Then she blamed herself: 'I'm wronging Ahmet's people,' she thought. 'They are not like my father. They would never take prisoner the guest, the suppliant. They would never touch a hair of a woman's head who came to them with a request.'

She went straight to Yusuf's room. He was sitting on a couch, sharpening an old sword and polishing it to bring out some old design and inscription on it.

He smiled at his sister.

'Gülbahar!' he said. 'Haven't you gone to bed yet? It's late.'

She went and sat beside him. Yusuf had a long narrow face, pale, as though it had never seen the sun. He was very tall.

He gave her a strange questioning stare. Gülbahar threw herself at his neck and began to weep. Yusuf did not move. Then he asked coldly:

'What's wrong Gülbahar? Why are you crying?'

'If anyone can help me it's you, Yusuf,' she said. 'Only you.'

Yusuf's large hazel eyes opened wide.

'What's wrong?' he repeated.

Gülbahar's lips trembled. She could not bring herself to speak.

'Only you can save me from death,' she said at last.

Yusuf was really alarmed now.

'Girl, what's the matter with you?' he shouted.

She began to speak very quickly:

'Father is going to have the prisoners put to death. We must stop it. Let us go to the mountain people and ask

59

them for the horse. They will give it to us, I know. Come, Yusuf, my brother, come with me to the mountain people.'

'But what's it to you?' Yusuf exclaimed, astounded. 'And besides, father is right. They're all traitors, he's right to have them executed. What do you care about them?' Then he broke off and stared at her fixedly. 'Or is it that . . . Gülbahar?' he cried. 'Speak, is it that . . .?'

'Yes, that's how it is,' she said in a faint whisper.

Yusuf leaped to his feet.

'That Ahmet, is it? Father will kill you for this! He'll kill you, Gülbahar! Kill you, kill you . . .'

He rushed round and round the room madly as though performing an ancient fire-worshipper's dance.

'He'll kill you,' he kept muttering in a frenzy. 'Father will kill you, kill you!'

His eyes were huge with fear. Gülbahar was alarmed.

'Yusuf, stop! Have you gone mad?'

He gave a long wild peal of laughter.

'You're the one who's gone mad! You, you . . . Father will kill you.'

She tried again:

'Yusuf, brother Yusuf,' she appealed, 'won't you help me get that horse back?'

'You're mad! Really quite quite mad . . .'

'But they'll be beheaded! Ahmet will die if the horse is not brought back. And I'll kill myself too.'

'Oh, Gülbahar, don't. Please please don't be mad. How can I go with you for the horse? Father will kill us both. Please, Gülbahar, give it up! Please . . .'

He seemed crazed with fear. Gülbahar was stunned.

'All right then,' she said taking his hands in hers. 'I ask

60

nothing of you, nothing except that you should tell no one. Not even mother . . . If Gülistan hears, or Gülriz, they'll kill me. You won't tell anyone, will you?'

'Would I ever!' he exclaimed. 'Father would hack you to pieces and throw each piece of you to the dogs. Would I ever tell a soul . . .? And you too, be careful, Gülbahar.'

Was this her brother Yusuf? This frightened thing, like a cowering bird shrinking under the cover of its wings? Gülbahar was dumbfounded. She had always known her brother for a cool-headed, valiant lad. How could she have been so mistaken? And now, what if Yusuf went and told her father everything? He was in such a panic, who knows what it might drive him to do.

She left him there, a statue of fear and dismay, and went back to her room.

*   *   *

Near the summit of Mount Ararat, on the south-western side, is a lake they call Lake Küp, no larger than a threshing-floor, intensely blue and set deep in the mountain side, like a well, surrounded by a mass of sharp red glinting rocks.

Every year at the first awakening of spring, the shepherds of Ararat gather at the lakeside. Throwing their sunpatterned felt cloaks on to the copper-coloured earth, they sit in a ring round the lake and take out their pipes. From sunrise to sundown they play the song of Ararat's wrath. The shepherds of Ararat have beautiful sad dark eyes and long slim fingers. Some of them have flowing golden beards.

As they play, a tiny white bird circles round and round above them. At close of day the piping stops. The shepherds disperse into the gathering gloom, and the tiny white bird wheeling above darts down to the lake and dips the tip of a wing into the deep blue water. Then it fades into the night like the shepherds. The water is slightly ruffled where the wing has touched it, and little ripples move in widening circles to break on the copper-coloured shore. Suddenly, the reflection of a large horse falls upon the surface of the lake to melt away almost at once.

*　　*　　*

Beyazit Castle stood on a great mass of rock that fell into the plain on the southern flank of the mountain, forming a steep precipice. The great caravan route cut through the plain, and smaller roads criss-crossed it here and there. Beyazit town with its earthen-roofed houses, spread east of the castle towards the foot of Mount Ararat.

At the foot of a towering rock white-haired Hüso's smithy burned all through the night sending out showers of sparks into the surrounding darkness. Sometimes sparks would pour out all through the night in a huge stream.

There were nights when Mahmut Khan, at peace with himself, would sit at the window of his room till morning and watch the river of sparks that flowed out of the smithy door.

Nobody knew how old Hüso was. Together with his five sons he worked in the smithy, forging fine swords, sharp, unbreakable and inlaid with gold. In all his life he had never deigned to step into the Pasha's castle, nor for that matter into any great mansion that belonged to a Bey. He did not keep the fast during Ramazan, never made the *namaz* prayers, nor did he conform to any prescribed ritual of the Moslem religion. Some people said that Hüso the smith was a secret fire-worshipper. He was known on certain nights to apply the bellows so forcefully that the interior of the forge and the darkness about its entrance became alive with sparks, and then to kneel before the fire and stretch out his arms in invocatory prayer.

Summer and winter he wore no other clothing than a thick homespun cloth wound about his loins and a red sash binding it at the waist.

Sick at heart Gülbahar sat at her window. The whole town was asleep. From the door of Hüso's smithy the showers of sparks poured out into the night.

And inside, from the hollow depths of the castle dungeon, came the faint notes of Sofi's pipe playing the wrath of Ararat. Far in the distance, somewhere on the plain of Beyazit a horse was whinnying madly, a persistent agitated cry of fear.

'Sofi,' Gülbahar called.

The piping stopped at once.

'Sofi's here my dear, your slave . . .'

'Sofi,' she said, 'there's so little time left . . . We have to prevent this . . . What can we do?'

'Nothing,' he replied. 'Nothing at all.'

'Suppose you should escape from here . . . Suppose you went and persuaded them to bring the horse back.'

'That's not possible,' Sofi said. 'Sofi's your slave, my silver-tongued beauty, but that horse shall never come back here.'

They stood silent for a while in the darkness of the night.

'But it can't, it can't happen,' she said at last in dull dead tones. 'How can such a thing come to pass? It's too cruel . . . It's a crime . . .' Her voice broke. 'Oh, how I wish this castle would crash down in ruins!'

'Down to the ground in utter ruin . . .' Sofi's soft voice joined in her lament.

'For a horse! All because of a horse four people will lose their lives. Is it worth it?'

'This castle will be destroyed,' Sofi replied. 'A thousand castles like this . . . For it's more than just a horse that's at stake.'

'Sofi, listen! I've thought of a way. Sofi, what if I should go to your people on the mountain? Shall I go? Shall I tell them Ahmet and Sofi want the horse to be brought back?'

'Oh no, you can't do that!' Sofi exclaimed.

'Then let me go to my father and entreat him to renounce his horse.'

'No, my beauty, no,' Sofi said. 'No, you mustn't do that. Is it worth it, just for a life? Ah, let Sofi be your slave, my lady, the slave of your clever tongue and honeyed voice, but don't do that. Let Sofi be a slave to your lovely hair, so bright . . . A slave to your soft doe eyes, to your grace and fairness. A slave to your fiery heart where love burns

64

as strong as Leila's love for Mejnun . . . There is nothing you can do. Your love is doomed. Nothing, nothing can help you. Ah, Sofi would die rather than see you like this . . . But it is better so for you, better that it should never be . . . Would that Sofi could sacrifice himself for the despair in your heart.'

'I know,' she said with a moan. 'I know that sooner or later my father will have us slain, Ahmet and me . . . Ah, but the time goes by so quickly, Sofi! Soon the day will be upon us . . . I won't live on after that. I'll kill myself upon your graves . . . Oh Sofi, Sofi, help us not to die!'

Sofi spoke not another word. Gülbahar went on talking hardly knowing what she was saying, but Sofi was like a stone now. Not a sound could be got out of him.

She turned away and as she left, Sofi clasped his pipe and began to play. On and on he played without stopping.

Gülbahar looked out of the window into the night and her eyes rested on Hüso's smithy. Deep rumblings sounded from the far lofty heights of Ararat and the huge mountain shuddered and panted.

A shower of sparks streamed out of Hüso's door into the night. The steady clang of the hammer alternated with the mountain's deep panting.

She could not keep still. There must be a way to save them. Her mind, her senses, her whole body were bent on finding a way. She looked for help even from the flying bird and the creeping serpent. She roamed through the castle with unseeing eyes and suddenly an idea came to her.

Hüso the smith

Hüso was a fire-worshipper, a magician! . . . A good man
. . . He might be able to help her.

At once she made her way to the smithy and slipped
inside through a shower of sparks. The forge was warm,
and Hüso as usual was naked from the waist up. He did
not seem surprised to see Gülbahar. His hand on the bellows, he turned and looked, and it was as though he had
been expecting her for a long time, such was the expression
that crossed his face. His eyes dropped back to the iron in
front of him and for a while he went on working the
bellows. Then he took the glowing iron from the fire,
placed it on the anvil and brought down the hammer.
Sparks blazed up from the iron, filling the whole forge.

At last he looked up and smiled.

'You are welcome, my lady Gülbahar,' he said.

His voice was so warm and encouraging that she felt
better at once. She told him first all about the horse.

'I know,' Hüso said.

Then she went on to speak of Ahmet, Sofi and Musa
Bey, and what her father was doing to them.

'I know,' Hüso said.

Unhesitatingly, she told him of her love for Ahmet, of
the dark passion that had taken hold of her. To this he
said nothing, but seemed to withdraw and become lost in
thought.

'Next week, on Saturday, Father is going to have them
beheaded on the tower,' Gülbahar said. 'Is there no way
to save them?'

Hüso made no reply. He remained deep in thought.
The glowing embers in the furnace slowly turned black,
the iron grew cold. It became stone-cold, and still Hüso
did not move.

A few cocks crew. At last he raised his head.

'Come back tomorrow night and we'll see . . . Maybe we'll think of something. Some way to save them.'

He had sent a ray of hope through her. As she went back the sun came up over the shoulder of Ararat, red and frosty. A keen wind was blowing down from the mountain; cold, brittle, with a crepitating sound.

It seemed to Gülbahar that the night would never come. She sat at the window and stared at the forge without blinking, waiting for the magic to work.

A flock of white birds would soar out of the smithy door, then another and another . . . The sky above the castle would be white with birds. And suddenly all the gates of the castle would fall open and Ahmet and Gülbahar would find themselves before Lake Küp on Mount Ararat, on the heights where the mighty eagles dwell. They would be holding hands. Their eyes would meet and they would smile. Then meet and smile once more . . . What magic did not Gülbahar imagine being worked in the smithy while she waited for the night to fall. How many times did she not see herself as the heroine in the song of Ararat's wrath, who found happiness in the end!

By sunset she was so exhausted, so faint with emotion it was as though she would never be able to move again. As the midnight cocks crew she dragged herself up, and holding on to the walls, her heart fluttering like a bird's, she made her way to the forge.

Hüso perceived that she was half dead with anxiety.

'Alas,' he thought. 'I never knew it was so bad. She's just melted away in a single day.'

Much as he had tried, Hüso had found no solution to Gülbahar's problem. But she was looking at him in such a way . . . To disappoint her now was out of the question.

'My daughter,' he said, 'I'll find a way to bring that horse back before the fated day. Only, you too must do something. You know the Sheikh of the Caravans who dwells down in yonder village on the great caravan route? Go to him at once, and see what he has to tell you.'

'I know the Sheikh of the Caravans,' Gülbahar said. 'But he never sees anyone . . .'

The Sheikh of the Caravans was very old. He had a long white beard that shone like snow under the sun. Day and night he sat on a large thick furry bearskin. Age had shrunk him into a tiny ball. In front of his house was a massive oak-tree, as holy as the Sheikh himself, perhaps even more so. Countless were the tales of the miracles worked through the saintly power of the Sheikh and the sacred tree. A little way off the great caravan route went by. All the roads coming from Arabia, from Trebizond, from the whole of Anatolia met here to run on to Iran and Turan, to India and China and beyond. And whoever the head of the passing caravan might be, of whatever nation or faith, he would never fail to put money, little or much, at the foot of the great oak-tree. Nobody would dream of touching the money left by these caravans. It would accumulate there, between the roots of the tree, and at *bayrams* and holy feasts the Sheikh would take it and distribute it to the poor. No caravan would have risked passing by without this oblation to the Sheikh's oak-tree. Frightening tales were told of the disastrous ends

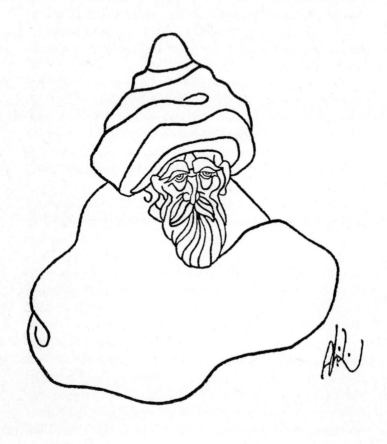

*The Sheikh of the Caravans consulting with the
blue-flaming star over his house*

that came to those who had neglected to do this . . . And every night, over the great oak-tree, Venus of the Caravans would sway gently in the sky, glistening softly till break of day, pointing the way to lost caravans and helping travellers in distress.

'You will tell him that I sent you,' Hüso said.

Gülbahar made for the Sheikh's dwelling at once. She kissed the holy tree and the threshold of his house and sent in Hüso's greetings. The Sheikh agreed to see her.

His blue eyes were like stars, his whole person like a clear unsullied spring. Gülbahar prostrated herself, then kissed him on the shoulder three times.

'I am yet another wayfarer, Sheikh,' she said kneeling before him, 'a wayfarer lost in the mountains and turning to you for help. My caravan has been caught in the storms of Mount Ararat. If you do not succour us, we will perish, my friends and I. I am a bird at its last gasp come to rest on the oak-tree in front of your house. Birds of prey are wheeling all about me with sharpened bills and open talons, ready to pluck my heart out . . .'

The Sheikh was moved by Gülbahar's distress and her great beauty.

'Tell me what is troubling you, daughter,' he said.

Gülbahar told him everything from the very beginning. When she had finished, the Sheikh buried his hands in his beard and fixed his eyes on Venus of the Caravans. The star glowed and glittered like a blue-flaming fire. So long did he remain motionless, plunged in meditation, that Gülbahar, still kneeling at his feet, felt her whole body growing numb.

At last he spoke.

'Go now, daughter,' he said, 'and know that things will

71

come to pass before Ahmet is beheaded, before he and
Sofi and Musa Bey lose their lives. One half of the star is
dim, but the other is still bright . . . Go, daughter, and
take with you my prayers for your happiness. Tell the
smith this: Something must be done about that horse.
Let Hüso come to me.'

Gülbahar left the Sheikh with her head in a whirl. The
tiny spark of hope in her had been fanned to a flame.

And so she waited in the castle, but as time passed and
nothing happened anguish overwhelmed her again. She
had faith in the power of the Sheikh and in the magic of
the votive tree. She believed in the star of the caravans
and trusted Hüso the smith. But as the day fixed for the
execution drew near, she could see her father's anger
growing ever more terrible. People shrank from ap-
proaching him and he spoke not a word to anyone. All
alone, in a ferment of rage, he nursed his smouldering
anger. His face was sallow and wasted, his shoulders
hunched under an invisible weight. Something was eating
away at him. There was something hurtful to his honour
in this business, but what, he himself did not know.

Gülbahar dared not visit the dungeon any more.
Memo's behaviour to her, that infinite indulgence shown
only to a sick demented helpless person, made her feel as
if all her pride were being trampled underfoot. He was
like a saint, ready to give up this world and its joys, or so
it seemed to Gülbahar, and that look in his eyes, so full of
grief and despair, and at once so sick with love . . . Surely
no one had ever looked like that at anyone, no one before

72

in this world. It was a look to pierce the hardest granite or steel, a look that stabbed you to the heart. All the sorrow and love in the world were concentrated in the eyes of this man with the face of a saint.

Since that night Gülbahar had been obsessed by the thought of Memo. He had done everything she had asked of him, at the risk of his life, like a man bewitched, as though there could be no greater pleasure or happiness for him. It seemed to her that if she but said, 'Memo, will you give me your life, will you die for me?' he would go mad with joy. Could it be that he had fallen in love with her? But then would he have allowed her to see Ahmet? Would he have helped her to meet him with every sign of happiness at doing something for her? His eyes shining, his whole body alive with infinite joy . . . Or was it infinite grief . . . ?'

'Memo, oh Memo, brother Memo, I shall never forget your goodness, your kindness, never till I die and my spirit leaves my body!'

And all the while she hovered outside the dungeon door, taking care not to be seen by Memo.

From the forge, masses of sparks poured out into the darkness. In the radiance of the frosty Ararat night, the stars, big and small, teemed in the sky. The silence was complete and the air quite still. And Gülbahar sat on at her window, sleepless, all through the night. Then as the day began to pale her heart leaped with joy. There, before the smithy, was a horse, saddled and waiting. In a moment Hüso emerged and, leaping on to the horse, galloped off into the mountain. Gülbahar knew where he was going. And now she was confident that the Pasha's horse would be returned to him.

The news spread through the countryside that Hüso the smith had gone to the mountain people to ask for the Pasha's horse, and everyone rejoiced. A man like Hüso, and carrying the Sheikh's seal too, would never be turned away empty-handed by the tribesmen, that was sure. There was not a man in these parts who did not respect the Sheikh, and no one would dare to set himself up against his seal.

Musa Bey's father and the other Kurdish Beys, when they heard the news, all rode into Beyazit town, followed by their horsemen clad in their goatskins and high felt caps. They were filled with relief and joy. And wonder too. How had the great remote Sheikh of the Caravans got mixed up in this affair? Who had told him that three people were about to lose their lives because of a horse? Everyone knew that the Sheikh of the Caravans had long since relinquished all ties with this world and its petty ways.

It was three days now to execution day. What if Hüso the smith had not returned by then? This was the thought that curbed their joy and cast a shadow over their hearts.

Mahmut Khan heard the news too and his rage knew no bounds. In his heart of hearts he cursed the Sheikh of the Caravans.

'Anyway,' he thought, 'it's too late. It can't be done by Saturday. And besides, the mountain people will never give up the horse. Why, those savage pig-headed brutes don't even know the Sheikh of the Caravans, let alone his seal! If he went and asked them himself, they'd still not give it to him. And even if they do . . . If they do give it up . . .'

Pacing up and down the great hall of the castle with its many pillars of coloured marble, Mahmut Khan could not contain himself.

'Even if they do . . .' he growled aloud. 'Even if they bring that horse back and tie it to the castle gate, I'll have them beheaded all the same on the bastion of the tower this Saturday. Yes, and throw their carcasses to the dogs. They are rebels who have defied Ottoman authority, and all for a horse too. Their blood shall flow at dawn this Saturday. I'll have their heads, even that miserable, mutinous, thousand-year-old Sofi's.'

And then on Thursday evening, Hüso returned, and he had the horse with him! He led it up to the castle and tied it to the big gate. A wave of joy swept through the town. People dressed in their best clothes and poured into the streets. The women tied gay-coloured scarves over their head-dresses.

Gülbahar was beside herself with joy. She rushed straight to the dungeon. Memo's face was haggard now, but Gülbahar saw nothing. His beautiful black eyes were drowned in grief, sunk in their sockets. It was as though he were afloat in a remote deserted world, all by himself. Weakly his hand went to the key at his waist, and as he gave it to Gülbahar it was as if he had no hands at all, as if the key had dropped into her hand of itself.

His legs weaving into each other, Memo walked away. At the castle gate he saw the horse, still tied up, its head

*The horse tied to the castle gate after Hüso the smith has
brought it back from Mount Ararat*

raised, sniffing the night air. Nobody had touched it since Hüso had brought it. Its harness gleamed dully in the darkness. Suddenly Memo came to himself. He looked at the horse with deadly hatred, fighting back the impulse to sever its head at one swift stroke of his sword. His hand on the hilt of the sword, in the grip of an overwhelming desire to kill, he stalked round and round the horse, his body bathed in sweat.

And in the old disused watch-turret that overhung the precipice just above the dungeon, Gülbahar and Ahmet were clasped in each other's arms. The night had drawn a golden cloud over them. They were lost to all the world now, swept up by the torrent of their great passion, as though, about to die, they had to compress a lifetime of love into one night, into one brief moment. A seething fire welded their bare bodies, and their blood coursed into each other's veins. Had they not come to the threshold of death, they would never have been joined together like this, in such a blaze of ecstasy.

Just before dawn Memo came upon them in the old watch-turret. They had wrapped themselves up in Ahmet's ample goatskin cloak and lay there as one body, in the darkling light of dawn. Memo's naked sword was still in his hand. His face ran with blood, for in his rage he had bitten his lips and ripped off whole tufts of his moustache.

In the first light of dawn Gülbahar's face wore a child-

77

like look of contentment. Memo stopped and gazed in wonder upon this face. His terrible rage subsided. He put the long sword back into its sheath and turned away.

It was not long before he found himself at the castle gate again, and once more the sight of the horse lashed him into frenzy. He whipped out his sword and wheeled round and round the horse, sweating, then whirled back and rushed up, sword in hand, to the very edge of the great precipice at the bottom of the castle. His mind was made up. One by one, he would fling open all the doors of the castle . . . One by one he would drag out the inmates and put them to the sword . . . Every single living creature . . . His legs took him back to the dungeon, and again to the door of the old watch-turret. Gülbahar's face was clearer now. Her lips were slightly parted. He could see her teeth, white like a child's. The dimples in her cheeks were more alluring than ever and her hair spread over Ahmet's face, hiding him.

Sword in hand, Memo stood looking at that face in wonder. He could go on gazing at her for a whole life-time, for a thousand years and still not have enough. Ah, but it was nearly day . . . Any time now they would wake up. How ashamed he was as he looked at her now, of his thoughts during the night. And still he could not take his eyes away. He gazed on and on as though he would never see her again, as though he were engraving her image indelibly on the very pupils of his eyes.

Sober and ashamed, Memo left them once more, but some strange force took him back to the horse, and the frenzied madness gripped him again. Many times he came and went, and each time Gülbahar's sleeping face seemed more beautiful in the growing light of dawn.

At last Gülbahar awoke. She saw the figure of a man with a naked sword bearing down upon them. She knew it was Memo and knew too what he meant to do. She pressed closer to Ahmet and waited. It was better that it should end this way. Ahmet had seen Memo too. He made no move at all, except to clasp Gülbahar more tightly. The same thought was in his mind. It was better this way. Their love had been doomed from the start.

The sword hung over them in the dawn light like a glistening drop of water. They held their breath, waiting for it to strike. Three times Memo, with all the strength in his body, flung the sword up, three times his arm dropped back. He knew they were awake and aware of what he was going to do. He had felt them draw more tightly together to await death in a last embrace.

He fled. Back he went to the castle gate. The sentinels were handing over the watch. He was beyond seeing anything. With the bare sword in his hand, he rushed back and forth from the horse to the dungeon and back again at a mad speed, and his huge sword cast lightning sparks into the air. Suddenly he dashed it down over the blue granite stone of the dungeon. The clangour resounded all through the castle and was heard way off in Beyazit town. The sword was shivered to pieces.

Quickly he went to the old watch-turret. He looked at them and all the old hero-worship was in his eyes. He was again the gentle, saintly Memo.

But he must rouse them. It was growing late.

'It's morning,' he said wearily. 'Wake up. Can't you see it's late?'

They were still clinging to each other, waiting for the fatal blow.

79

Memo the jailer holding his sword over the lovers
like a glistening drop of water

'It's day already,' Memo repeated. 'Come, get up before someone sees you. Hurry.'

He left them and the lovers emerged from under their golden cloud of love. Gülbahar ran to the castle gate. The horse was there, standing at ease, waiting. The silver and gold of its trappings sparkled in the first rays of the sun. Gülbahar turned to the rising sun and stretched out her arms joyfully.

The horse had come back. And now Ahmet would go. She would never see him again, never. A whole lifetime of happiness would have gone into those brief hours of love . . . All her life she would look back and live again the bliss of this one night.

'Thanks be to the rising sun, to the bright mountain . . . Thanks be to the Creator,' she said. 'I am grateful for the little that I have been given.'

The sun was up at the height of a minaret when the Kurdish Beys began to arrive at the castle. Slowly they came in ones and twos, looking cheerful, standing very straight, their long massive swords hanging from their waists. Each newcomer walked round the horse and looked it over with care and deference before entering the castle. From the vast many-pillared court of the castle came the sound of angry shouting.

'That's not my horse,' Mahmut Khan was saying. His face was yellow and he was quivering with rage. 'With all due respect to the Sheikh, I tell you it's not my horse. And for that reason I shall have them all beheaded tomorrow Saturday at dawn.'

Mustafa Bey, the Bey of the Zilan tribe attempted to argue with him.

'But Pasha,' he said, 'that horse is yours. I should know . . .'

This was enough to lash the Pasha to fresh fury.

'Bey! Mustafa Bey, be careful! Or are you one of those rebels too? You too . . .?'

The other Beys intervened quickly.

'Pasha,' they said, 'it's something else he meant to say. You misunderstood him . . .'

'I? I, misunderstood someone? What do you mean? I? Not understand anything . . .?'

'Far be it, Pasha! We ask your pardon,' they said. 'It's we who misunderstood you. Would you ever misunderstand anything!'

After that not one of them opened his mouth to say another word. All their joy was blighted.

'Yes, Beys,' the Pasha repeated. 'Tomorrow morning at break of day, those thieves who stole my horse and have not brought it back shall die. Their heads shall fall on the bastion of the tower before the eyes of all good Ottoman subjects. I am sending out my heralds at once to cry the news in the town market.'

The Kurdish Beys bowed themselves out of the Pasha's presence, revolt smouldering in their hearts. Outside, they gathered around the horse and examined it.

'It's his horse,' one of them said at last. 'I'll swear to it.'

'It's his emblem blazoned on the saddle-cloth.'

'Then why does he insist on having them beheaded? What has the Pasha got against these three men?'

'Let him have them beheaded then! Retribution won't wait for Judgment Day.'

'That it won't!' the Beys roared all together.

The heralds were out in the market-place announcing the names of the condemned men and proclaiming their crimes. Soon the news was all over Beyazit town.

Hüso the smith went mad with rage. Like one of the Furies he rushed to the castle gate, brandishing his hammer and shouting at the top of his voice.

'Tyranny! Oppression! Pasha, you won't get away with this. Your tyranny won't last for ever. The horse is yours, Pasha. You're not worthy of it, but still the horse is yours. Does Hüso lie? I brought it back to you, Pasha. I should know . . .'

Suddenly he threw himself at the horse, untied the halter from the iron ring of the gate and set it loose.

'You're not worthy of this horse, Pasha! You're not even worthy of being called a man! You . . . You . . . You're unworthy . . .'

Unrestrained, the horse drifted off into Beyazit town, wandering from house to house, from shop to shop, until it came to the town square. There it paused, threw up its head and sniffed long and hard at the air. Suddenly it neighed loudly with a sound that echoed back from Ararat Mountain. Waving its tail it reared on its hind legs several times as though about to take wing, then it galloped off towards the mountain at full speed and vanished up the slope like a shooting star.

People shuddered as they heard the horse's neigh.

'That Pasha will come to a bad end,' they said.

Up in the castle the executioners were sharpening their big heavy broadswords and making their preparations for the morrow.

Gülbahar was frantic with grief. All that day she roamed like a wraith through the castle, and as soon as night fell, she slipped away to the forge.

'What can we do, my daughter?' was all Hüso could say. 'We tried but it was no use. There's nothing more we can do. Not even the Sheikh can be of any help now. It was fated this way, what can we do . . .'

Silently, the tears streaming down her face, Gülbahar turned away.

'I'll give him poison . . . ' she thought fiercely. 'The deadly poison that kills a man at one strike before he can run from the sunshine into the shade. I won't let him live on after this!'

She went back to the castle. Perhaps Yusuf could do something. But when she found him he would not even talk to her and cast her such a stern hostile look that she was dumbfounded. She went to find the steward of the castle, Ismail Agha. The Pasha, she knew, had great faith in Ismail Agha's counsel and loved him too. Perhaps . . . But Ismail Agha, in a black mood, was unapproachable. Her mother . . . ? Even her mother seemed hostile to her. She could not bring herself to go near her. Everyone in this castle, every single thing was against her, the walls, the marble pillars, the Kurdish rugs that covered the floors, even the huge white Van cats she loved so much, with one eye blue and the other golden yellow. They looked at her with hate now.

She picked up the kitten that had grown up on her lap and in her bed. Its blue and gold eyes flashed.

'My little pussycat,' she wept, cradling it in her arms. 'My white golden-eyed pussy, there's only you I can tell. Only you I can pour out my heart to. They are going to kill him, my Ahmet, my only love. The eagle of the high mountains, the lord of my heart . . .'

On and on she mourned. The cat in her arms was a soft purring ball now. She felt a great darkness encompassing her, a wall of despair against which she beat her head and strained and struggled.

'Tomorrow morning they will strike off his head. Oh my little pussycat, they will kill him, do you hear me? But I won't live on after him. I'll kill myself too, my little pussycat . . .'

Still holding the cat, as though walking in her sleep she drifted towards the dungeon. The cat was warm in her arms and its purring grew louder.

The dungeon gate was cold. Memo, the jailer, was standing beside it leaning on a huge sword. He was wrapped in a short deerskin cloak that stopped at the knees. His long beautiful face, his black eyes, his curly ebony beard were plunged in sorrow.

'And I too . . . Tomorrow morning, as they strike his head off and cast his body over the precipice, I shall leap to my death after him.'

She was beside herself and did not realize that Memo had heard her words.

'Oh Memo, Memo! You have been so good to me . . . Let me see him one last time.'

Gülbahar talks to Memo in secret

Then suddenly in broken strangled tones she spoke again as in a trance.

'Memo, let him go! Set him free. Let him go. For my sake . . . Can't you? Not for my sake? Am I nothing to you?'

She dropped the cat and clasped Memo's hands, and it was as though she had cast a spell over him.

'Memo, oh Memo, you have a huge deadly sword in your hand. You have black, flaming eyes, clever fingers . . . You are tall and strong . . . And yet Memo . . . My brother Memo, of what use have all these been to you? To be just the keeper of a jail? To please a Pasha? To strike off people's heads? Memo, Memo! Oh Memo, let him go. I'll give you anything . . .'

Such a deep agonizing moan escaped him that Gülbahar was shaken out of her trance-like state.

'You will give me anything?' he said.

'Anything you ask of me I'll give you, Memo. My valiant Memo! My brother Memo . . .'

'You will give me anything I ask of you?' he said again.

'Ask for my soul and I'll give it you,' Gülbahar said, fear and curiosity sounding in her voice. 'Whatever you ask for, Memo, I'll give you. Only let Ahmet be saved.'

Memo was silent. He stood dazed, transfixed, his face shining with happiness in the faint light of the candle. Then he smiled. He put out his hand to her hair and stroked it very gently as though afraid it might break. Gülbahar waited, wondering, fascinated, her body tense and still.

When Memo spoke again, it was with the ease, the serenity, the bliss of a man whose every wish in this world has been granted. His voice was vibrant with joy.

'You will give me anything I ask for?'

'Yes, I will,' she said firmly, fervently. 'I will, Memo.'

'Then I am asking you. Give me a lock of your hair.'

Swiftly she held out one of her many little braids.

'Draw your sword and cut it off, Memo,' she said. 'It is yours with Gülbahar's blessing.'

Memo unsheathed the sword and cut a small lock from the tip of the braid. He put it into his breast.

'I want something else,' he said.

'Speak, ask and it shall be yours,' she said unhesitatingly.

'I wish that Gülbahar should never forget me, never forget this night and what has taken place. I want her to remember all her life.'

Gülbahar clasped his hands. He drew away from her and went to the dungeon.

'Ahmet, Musa Bey, Sofi, wake up . . .'

They were awake and rose to their feet. Memo unlocked their iron fetters.

'Go through that gate down there. You have only till break of day. You must get well away before that or they will catch you.'

Ahmet saw Gülbahar outside. He went to her and took her in his arms.

'Hurry!' she said. 'Oh hurry, hurry! It's not long to dawn. The guards will catch you.'

They parted and the three prisoners left the castle through the lower gate of the dungeon.

Gülbahar watched them go. Then she turned to Memo, but he had disappeared. She went looking for him, but he was nowhere to be found.

Morning came. The rays of the sun crept down the slopes of Mount Ararat and lengthened into Beyazit town and Beyazit Castle, pale, sad, victorious, triumphant . . .

The executioners appeared at the dungeon.

'Open the door, Memo,' they called, 'and get the condemned men ready.'

As though nothing untoward had happened Memo smiled.

'I set them free last night,' he said blandly.

Incredulous, they went to look in the dungeon themselves and could not believe their eyes. Not one of the prisoners was there. They ran to the Pasha at once.

Mahmut Khan clapped his hand to his sword and rose. Ismail Agha, his men, the army captains rose too as one man. Their hands on their swords they trooped after the Pasha and followed him to the dungeon.

Memo was waiting for them, alone, his sword in his hand. He laughed.

'I set them free last night, Pasha,' he said calmly. 'Didn't I do right? I thought you would be pleased.'

'Dog!' the Pasha roared. 'Is this how you repay me? After all I've done for you?'

He lunged at Memo. The others fell upon him too with furious violence, yet not one of them succeeded in drawing near. Memo kept them all at bay as they attacked him in ever greater numbers, brandishing their swords. Fighting, Memo retreated up to the bastion of the tower where the condemned men were to have been beheaded that morning at this very hour. There, on the edge of the precipice, he stopped.

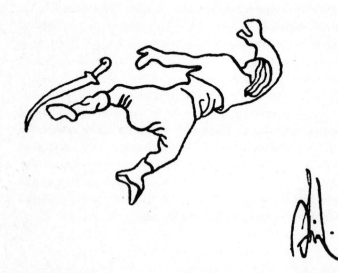

Memo's body lying at the bottom of the deep chasm
like a broken bird

'Pasha,' he said, 'Pasha, I could keep you all here fighting for three days and three nights too . . . But what's the use . . . I've had my heart's desire. I am content and want no more of this world. What if I fight on and kill a few of your men? What difference will it make to you or to me? So farewell . . . Farewell to those I leave behind. Farewell to those who love me . . . Or love me not!'

And he hurled himself from the bastion of the tower. From above, Memo's body, lying at the very bottom of the precipice, looked like a broken bird with one of its wings open.

Hüso, the smith, was the first to reach him. Then his sons came. Then the women, the young girls . . . A cry of lamentation rose over Beyazit town. Hüso knelt beside the dead man and kissed his brow. Memo's left hand was clenched tight and lay over his heart. Hüso forced the fingers open with his strong hands. A lock of black hair, bright and fiery, gleamed in the sun and slid on to the tender green grass.

Yusuf had followed the events of the past few hours with horror and a growing fear. He had seen the pool of blood on the green grass. He had seen the horse rearing in Beyazit town.

Everyone knew that the horse was the Pasha's horse and no other. Why then had he refused to recognize it? Could it be . . .? Could it be that his father knew all? All about what Gülbahar had done? Was that the reason why?

Ah, he knew! He knew everything. Was it possible that

he shouldn't? The Pasha could see through the thickest wall, could even hear what was spoken in far-off places . . . Could anyone deny this? Yes, he knew what Gülbahar had done. He knew everything.

Why had Memo killed himself? Out of fear? But he could have run away after having set the prisoners free, couldn't he? But where would he have gone? Anywhere, up into the mountains or to the castle of the Bey of Hoshap, anywhere . . . Ah, the Pasha would have found him out in the end wherever he tried to hide. He would have had him skinned alive.

Once, Yusuf was only a child, but how could he forget the man mounted backwards on a donkey, stark naked, with only a cloth to hide his private parts, being led through the town square by a creature with rheumy lashless eyes and red raw flesh where the lashes had been. And the two colossal men, the two executioners, one on each side . . . The huge broadsword dripping with blood in the hand of one and the small glinting dagger held by the other . . . Yusuf saw it all again as clearly as if it were happening now. The executioner with the dagger put out his hand, seized the left ear of the man huddling on the donkey, his arms bound with stiff rope, and sliced it off at the root. He looked at the ear, then at the watching crowd and laughed and laughed. The voice of the man on the donkey rose in a long agonizing cry. He writhed and the rope cut into his arms. Blood spurted from where the ear had been. The executioner pitched the severed ear far out over the heads of the onlookers. It dropped in front of a shop. The shopkeeper, a hefty man with an eagle nose and a round black beard, stood staring, transfixed, at the bloody ear that had fallen into his shop and lay there oozing blood. Fixedly he stared, never moving, never batting an eyelid.

The donkey was streaming with blood. The second executioner was stripping the naked man's skin with his keen broadsword. He did it as neatly as if he were fleecing a sheep. The man had no voice left. Only a rattling sound came out of him.

A vast crowd had collected, but people's faces showed no horror. It was not an unusual occurrence.

In the afternoon they brought the man to the castle gate and threw him on to the stone paving. There was no end to the blood that flowed out of him. The whole town, its houses, its shops, its streets were steeped in blood. Blood gushed out of the earth itself.

That night Yusuf was sick. He vomited till morning. All the children of Beyazit town were sick and vomiting too. The odour of blood was everywhere.

Yusuf's mother was weeping at his bedside.

'He'll get used to it,' the Pasha consoled her. 'He'll have to or how will he live in this world and bear its ways?'

His mother wept on, uncontrollably. Then Yusuf had fainted. He remembered nothing more.

After that day he had seen many men mounted backwards on donkeys. He had got used to it. He had seen countless heads fall before his eyes on the bastion of the castle tower, countless men beaten with chains in the town square. He had also seen his father at such moments, with rigid face and glittering eyes, growing taller and broader, swelling into an unfamiliar awesome figure, who had power to create or destroy. At such moments his father was the god of wrath erupting from Mount Ararat in a burst of thunder and lightning.

Yusuf lived in dread of his father. To him he was not a father but an instrument of terror.

That night he could not sleep, and the more sleep eluded him the more intense became his fear. He was convinced now that his father knew Gülbahar had confided in him and was only biding his time. His father never showed anything he felt, neither his anger nor his fear – did he know the meaning of fear? – neither his love nor his hate.

Suppose I run away, Yusuf thought . . . Suppose I go to Hoshap Castle and throw myself at the Bey's feet and beg and plead with him not to give me up. Hide me, I'll say, or if you can't, send me south to the Arabs of the desert where the black-eyed gazelles run free . . . But the Bey of Hoshap fears my father too . . . Everyone fears him, even the Shah and the Padishah . . . Only that wretched Gülbahar is not afraid of him, and Hüso the smith. What about the Sheikh of the Caravans . . . ? No, even he fears the Pasha.

All through the night these thoughts obsessed him. What if his father knew . . . ? What if he said, my own son was aware of all these goings-on and he never told me! He dared defy me! I must make an example of him in the town square or die myself. I must have his eyes gouged out. He shall be skinned alive . . . Or I will die.

By the morning Yusuf had worked himself into such a panic that he expected the executioners to come for him at any moment. Now, he said, now they'll be here with chains to bind me . . . There was a tiny little room near the castle pantry. Three men could barely have squeezed into it . . . He shut himself up in this room and held his breath. They would be looking for him now. They would search all through the castle and, not finding him, would dispatch horsemen to scour the countryside. The news would spread far and wide, that the Pasha's son had run away. There would be talk and scandal . . .

He shuddered, yet he did not move from his hiding-place. A ray of light filtered through a chink in the door. It dwindled and faded and Yusuf knew that it was night. He heaved a sigh of relief. He was saved for today. As he tiptoed out of the room a group of servants bowed low, without looking at him. It's a trap, Yusuf panicked again, a trap set by my father. He'll have me arrested now, this minute . . . His heart drumming in his ears, his stomach rumbling with hunger he flung himself into the kitchen.

There was a feeling of spring in the air. He caught the sharp scent of a distant flower. Then his nostrils tingled with the fumes of roasting meat. The servants had all jumped to their feet as he entered. He drifted through the kitchens, hungry, but too ashamed to ask for food. From the Council chamber came his father's voice, loud, boom-ing, angry. Abruptly it was silent, as though at the stroke of a knife. Yusuf hurried out into the courtyard of the castle. In the sentry-box a sentry with fierce-looking whiskers stood stiff and still as a post. Yusuf scurried into the castle mosque and crouched there, panting, like a hunted animal. Then again he was on his feet, making for the harem. He had to unburden himself. He would tell his mother everything. Anyway, he was dying of hunger.

His mother started up in alarm.

'What's the matter, Yusuf?' she cried. 'Are you sick?'

'I'm sick,' he said, with a moan, and sank on to his mother's bed.

He was indeed in a high fever.

For three days and three nights he lay there unconscious and delirious. Physicians were summoned from all over the countryside to treat him. His hands were tightly clenched.

On the evening of the third day he opened his eyes. His hands relaxed and the fingers unfolded.

When he was able to leave his bed he was like a frightened deer, trembling on his feet. He must tell his father, tell him the whole truth as he knew it. Suddenly it came to his mind that Gülbahar, his sister, so clever, so wise, must surely have a plan in mind to save herself. At once he ran to the harem.

Gülbahar was in her room, sitting at her spinning-wheel. The hum of the spinning-wheel irritated Yusuf.

'Gülbahar,' he blurted out. It was a cry of agony and fear.

'What is it, Yusuf?' she asked, but her voice was dull and absent.

'Father will gouge our eyes out. He will skin us alive. Father knows everything.'

'Have you gone and told him?'

'No, but he knows all the same. He will have us blinded, Gülbahar! Gouge our eyes out! Our eyes . . .'

'Then who could have told him?'

'I don't know. But I'm sure of it. Let's run away. Gülbahar, come let's flee . . .' He was clinging to her, his legs set wide apart, his chin quivering, rigid with terror. 'He knows, Gülbahar. Let's escape!'

'But where can we go?'

'Anywhere, oh anywhere away from him!'

Gülbahar made him sit on the couch.

'Wait a minute,' she said. 'Why should we run away?

And 'where would we go? Wait a minute. Think!'

'Father's setting a trap for you. He doesn't want you to know yet that he knows everything, how you went to Hüso the smith, how you persuaded him to bring that horse back. Why, I myself saw you enter the smithy! Wouldn't father know? Of course he does! He knows all about you and Ahmet too. Why, he even knows that we're together here right now, you and I. He sees everything, he knows all. If we don't escape, he'll gouge our eyes out, he will. I heard him talking to Ismail Agha . . .'

'What was he saying?'

'He said, I'll kill them both, brother and sister. I'm just waiting to see if Yusuf will decide to confess all to me, if Gülbahar will repent and beg my forgiveness. I'll wait today too . . . Tomorrow, I'll have them clapped in the dungeon.'

Everything was clear to Gülbahar now. For many years she herself had harboured this same sensation, that her father knew everything and saw all; it was very difficult to get rid of this feeling once it had got hold of you, however much you reasoned about it. Yusuf's case was hopeless. Sooner or later he would go to the Pasha and tell him everything. Or else he would drop dead in a paroxysm of fear. It was terror that had prevented him from giving her away up to now. She saw clearly how it was going to be. The Pasha would know at once that it was she, Gülbahar, who had arranged for the prisoners' escape. He would know too who had sent Memo to his death. Why should Memo let those three men go? Why should he give up his life in this way? Wouldn't her father ask himself that?

Yusuf's face was all yellow and taut.

'I'm going,' he said suddenly.

He banged the door and made straight for the Council chamber. The Pasha was there together with Ismail, the Provost-Marshal and two Kurdish Beys. There were also some strange dervishes who must have come from a far land. Two soldiers were on guard at the door.

Yusuf rushed up to the Pasha and clasped his hands.

'Father, forgive me. Don't kill me, don't gouge my eyes out! You know all, you've seen everything. Forgive me. I was never a traitor to you. Forgive me . . .'

And in one breath the whole story was out, how Gülbahar had come to him, what she had proposed that they should do, how she had gone to the smith and afterwards to the Sheikh of the Caravans. He told the Pasha everything he knew, without leaving out a single thing.

'And now hurry! Catch her before she runs away,' he said. 'She may be gone already . . .'

A lightning flash went through the Pasha's head and everything became clear. Memo's treachery had been a baffling blow to him. It had driven him mad with anger, and with sorrow too for he had loved Memo as a son.

He lurched to his feet, livid, his two arms opening out at his sides like the wings of an eagle. He swayed and would have fallen, had he not leaned against the wall, his lips suddenly dry and cracked, his beard quivering. Then he slumped back on to the couch. His hands went to his breast.

Everyone had left the room except Ismail Agha. Yusuf lay crumpled up on the floor near the couch.

The Pasha spoke at last.

'Ismail Agha, what is this? How can it be? Our honour, our good name trampled underfoot! That Gülbahar

98

should do such a thing . . . So Memo? Ha? So that sorceress cast a spell upon him . . . She never gave a thought to our honour and good name. She disgraced her rank! Never before has such a calamity fallen upon our house, never, Ismail Agha! Ah, we have been too lax . . . But no one must hear of this, Ismail Agha, no one, or I shall be shamed throughout the land of the Ottomans. Yet I don't understand. Why did she do this? Who is she in love with? Ahmet? If so, what about Memo? Memo . . .'

Somehow Mahmut Khan would not believe that his daughter, his own daughter, could stoop to the other possibility that came to his mind. He rose.

'Ismail Agha,' he said. 'No one must hear of this. And the girl, we must make away with her at once, this instant.'

'No,' Ismail Agha said. 'People will be quick to link that with Memo.'

'Then what shall we do, Ismail Agha? We must deal with her somehow or other.'

'Let me think,' Ismail Agha said.

There was a long silence.

'Shall we pretend we don't know and wait awhile?' Mahmut Khan suggested.

'No,' Ismail Agha said. 'There is no way to hold her. She will run off in the end. Except . . . Either we do away with her secretly . . . Or no, we can shut her up in the dungeon. In that deep pit where we once threw Ali Bey . . .'

'That's what we'll do,' the Pasha decided. 'Only put a good trusty man to guard her, or we'll have trouble again . . .'

'Don't worry, Pasha.'

Gradually, the Pasha recovered his self-possession.

99

A lightning flashed through the Pasha's head . . .

Everything was clear now, the affair of the horse, Sofi and his pipe-playing, everything was as clear as daylight. It was plain that Gülbahar's relations with Ahmet must date from a long while ago.

Ismail Agha made straight for Gülbahar's room, taking two men with him.

She was waiting. After Yusuf had left her she knew it would not be long before Ismail Agha and the executioners came for her. She was ready, standing, her head held high. Ismail Agha made a sign and the two men seized hold of her. Then he led the way down to the dungeon and came to the pit. It was empty.

'Help the Lady Gülbahar down,' Ismail Agha ordered. He was careful not to be lacking in respect.

Gülbahar refused to be supported and descended the steep steps alone.

Ismail Agha locked the trapdoor with his own hand and pocketed the key.

'You will both of you mount guard here,' he said to his men. 'And if she escapes it will be at the price of your head.'

The Pasha had summoned his wife and appraised her of the whole affair.

'The boy is quite spent,' he said pointing to Yusuf who was still lying in a crumpled heap beside the sofa. 'I fear for his health. Nurse him well. And remember, no one but you must know where that girl is. When Yusuf comes to his senses, you will impress upon him that he is not to breathe a word of all this to anyone.'

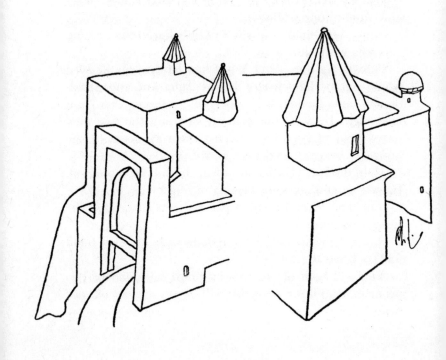

The dungeon of Beyazit Castle

Then he lifted Yusuf on to the sofa beside him and stroked his head.

'My own valiant son,' he said as he caressed him. 'You have proved yourself worthy of your noble blood. You would not have us dishonoured and disgraced . . .'

Yusuf was slowly regaining his senses.

'You are not going to kill me?' he whispered, his eyes opening huge, dazed with fear. 'You are not going to gouge my eyes out?'

The Pasha kissed him on the brow.

'What are you talking about?' he said. 'You have been brave and loyal, and for that I shall make you a gift of a handsome sword or whatever weapon you desire, and of a noble steed too. What are you saying? Why should I kill you?'

Yusuf was weeping now with relief and exhaustion.

'Hatun,' the Pasha said, 'take him away. He is not himself. He has had a great fright.'

She took Yusuf by the arm and led him out of the room.

Ismail Agha was waiting outside. He entered as soon as they left.

'It's done, my Pasha,' he said.

'Nobody must know. Nobody must hear of this, Ismail Agha.'

'We shall do what is necessary, Pasha.'

'I feel easier now, Ismail Agha. The whole affair didn't make sense. It worried me. It preyed on my mind . . . We'll let some time pass, Ismail Agha, and then deal with that girl.'

'That's easy, Pasha. But we mustn't be hasty. Let everything be forgotten, and then . . .'

Yet no amount of caution and secrecy could prevent the news from leaking out in a very short time. At first nobody believed it. That the Lady Gülbahar should be cast into the deep pit of the dungeon! It was impossible!

Hüso the smith heard the news too. And so did the Sheikh of the Caravans. But for them it was no more than they had expected.

The story spread all over Mount Ararat, then to the shores of Lake Van, to Erzurum, and Kars, and Erzincan, and the love of Gülbahar and Ahmet became a legend on everyone's tongue. Bards composed songs about the girl in the pit of Beyazit dungeon and the minstrels and pipers set them to music.

A pall of mourning fell over the whole of Ararat. Youths and warriors and newly-wed young brides wept. 'How can we be happy?' they said. 'How can we ever look each other in the face while she is rotting in that black pit?'

Ahmet, the Sheikh of the Caravans, Hüso the smith, the people of Mount Ararat and of Erzurum plain, did not sleep for nights on end, their consciences bleeding, anger and shame swelling like a festering wound in their breasts as the days went by.

Mount Ararat in its grandeur is like another world piled on top of this world. Most of the year its summit is hidden by clouds, but sometimes the clouds are replaced by masses of storm-tossed whirling stars. And when the sun, after the long Ararat night, emerges from over the mountain, it is a blood-red mass of glowing embers.

At night Mount Ararat looms larger and bulkier, as though it has swallowed up the rest of the world. The immense stillness is rent by formidable rumblings that echo and re-echo up and down the desolate slopes of the mountain. Even on the darkest night Mount Ararat never fades into the darkness. Like another night, blacker and lonelier, it marches upon the rest of the universe. But if there is a moon, then the mountain sways gently, a tenuous glimmering wraith. Mount Ararat is a fearsome sight at night. Its darkness is like a wall. And on sombre starless nights the rumblings that come from the mountain rise from very deep down, as though from out of a thousand years past, a dull, muted booming.

In the darkness, thick and dense as a stone wall, Mount Ararat seemed to stir. The stillness was complete, like the stillness before a storm.

And then the night, the darkness itself moved. The hard skin of the mountain quivered and on the slopes of the night an urgent angry tumult arose. Ahmet was on the horse, leading, and beside him all the people of Ararat were marching. The houses, the villages, were left behind empty. As they marched, pebbles slipped down the slopes and with them the mountain people streamed into Beyazit town.

At the same time on the shores of Lake Van and in the villages of the plain, people were roused too. From out of the skies, from the bowels of the earth, more and more people sprang up, and together with the night, together with the angry mountain, they marched upon the castle of Mahmut Khan.

As the sun rose and stole over one of Ararat's outlying ridges, Mahmut Khan seemed to see in a vision a vast crowd, some on horseback, some afoot, wrapped in the skins of goats and sheep and deer and colts, very tall men, some swarthy, some golden-haired, with clear blue eyes, fine hands, long necks, large eyes . . . From out of the shades of the night, the crowds emerged and Mahmut Khan closed his eyes.

When he opened them again, the mists were slowly lifting and the crowds of people were greater than before. And then he saw Ahmet on the horse. He swung around angrily to give an order. Then his mouth went dry and he stopped and thought. If the whole of Beyazit town with its stones and earth were turned into soldiers, what would it avail against a multitude such as this? One end reaching into Beyazit plain and the other end still up somewhere on the heights of Mount Ararat.

Slowly, steadily the people approached the castle. Like so many ants . . . Not a sound came out of them, not a word. Suddenly, a loud crash shattered the silence. The great gate of the castle had collapsed and the crowd was streaming in. Still silent, unhurried, they closed in on the dungeon.

Ismail Agha had already released Gülbahar and was standing with her beside the open trapdoor, trembling. Gülbahar blinked, dazzled by the rising sun, unable to discern anything, knowing only that she had been taken out of the pit, but for what?

Without a sound, without a word the people gathered Gülbahar up into their midst and flowed back out of the gateway.

Beside the tomb of Ahmedi Hani, the saint and poet, a great fire had been lit, and over its embers, which spread as wide as a threshing floor, dervishes and *sufis* were walking. All around them on the edge of the burning embers stood the novices, some chanting hymns and litanies for the fire-walkers, others playing on the pipe.

Still silent, bearing Gülbahar along, the crowd came to a standstill around the fire. They covered the slopes of Ararat, and even from a distance the fire-walkers could be seen, their bare sweating bodies springing out of the glowing embers like drops of water.

'I am a coward,' Mahmut Khan cried.

With naked sword, singly, he attempted to throw himself at the crowd. Ismail Agha and his attendants held him back. Again and again the Pasha struggled to free himself from their grasp.

'How can I live on after this?' he groaned. 'How, after having let the name of the glorious Ottoman be dragged in the mire? How, after being shamed and disgraced in the eyes of all the world? How? What can life hold for me after this . . .?'

But what a crowd! No force on earth could hold out against it. No army could overpower it . . . That horse had indeed turned out to be a scourge, Mahmut Khan was thinking.

The crowd remained massed beside the tomb of Ahmedi Hani, celebrating till sundown. To the wild beating of the drums, the dervishes performed traditional dances, half-naked, their feet flying over the burning embers, their

107

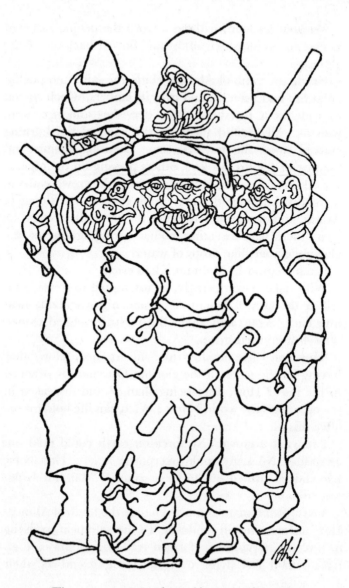

The vast angry crowd marching upon the castle

hands and feet whirling, their long hair fanning out like umbrellas.

Youths and maidens linked arms for the *gövend* dance and never before had anyone seen a *gövend* so gracefully danced. The long row of dancers, a man and a woman in turn, stretched right up to the castle itself. Seven drummers and seven fifers, all playing the same tune, were barely enough for this long line of dancers. The women wore aprons of embroidered silk. Their bright conical coifs streamed like the sun. And the *gövend* was like a sea, lapping at the foot of Ararat, its waves swelling, then ebbing, then seething with foam.

Gülbahar was taken to the house of Hüso the smith. There the women washed and bathed her and arrayed her in a beautiful gown of old Lahore cloth, a fairy-tale garment that seemed to have been fashioned without thread or needle. Then she was set upon her father's horse and taken to the Sheikh of the Caravans. Ahmet followed on another horse.

They knelt before the Sheikh and kissed him on both shoulders. And the Sheikh blessed them and kissed them too.

All these things took place in full view of the Pasha, and what he could not see was reported to him instantly.

This is what the Sheikh said:

'Mahmut Khan is an Ottoman, an infidel. Those people are cruel and inhuman. He will never forgive us for this and will bring trouble upon the people of Ararat. At the very least, he will have the villages raided and decimated. Let us therefore keep to the ancient tradition. Let it not be said that we too have broken the old customs. Ahmet, you are to take Gülbahar and go at once to Hoshap Castle, to the Bey. I shall give you my counsellor,

Ibrahim, to accompany you. The Bey of Hoshap Castle knows Ibrahim. Go and claim sanctuary with him and he will champion your cause, for he is one of my followers.'

It was an age-old tradition. If a young man abducted a girl and then sought asylum in a house, the head of this house must never return the girl to her father, whoever he might be. At whatever cost, he must obtain the father's consent, pay for the bridegroom's portion and arrange the wedding. Much blood had been shed over such elopements.

So now Gülbahar and Ahmet were going to the Bey of Hoshap Castle. This Bey was not entirely independent, but even if the abducted girl had been the daughter of the Ottoman Sultan and not just the Pasha's, he would never have refused her asylum. The old tradition forbade it. He would fight, risk his possessions, his title, even his life, but he would not surrender the runaway couple, for if ever he did such a thing, he would be disgraced in the eyes of the people, an object of contempt throughout the countryside.

Hoshap Castle, a beautiful fortress girded by three impregnable ramparts, in circles one within the other, stood on high steep crags that fell away to the great caravan road on the plain east of Lake Van. At the foot of the crags flowed the clear Hoshap River. No one knew when this fortress had been built. It had existed for centuries, and for centuries new wings had been added to it. Yet this had not impaired the harmony of the whole. The Bey of Hoshap could boast of being lord of the most beautiful castle in the world.

Gülbahar and Ahmet dismounted at the foot of the crags. The horses were taken to the stables of the Bey's soldiers in the village. The sentry, recognizing Ibrahim, saluted him and led them all up to the castle.

The Bey of Hoshap listened to the story as told him by Ibrahim.

'This Mahmut Khan knows neither custom nor tradition,' he said when Ibrahim had finished. 'He is a Bey no longer, but a Pasha now, an Ottoman. He is quite capable of marching upon us with all his soldiers when he learns that these children have come here. But there's no other way, we shall ask his consent for his daughter in all good faith, offer him all our goods and property if need be. The Sheikh's word is law to us. We are ready even to give up our life.'

And he clapped his hands for his attendants.

'Show our guests to their apartments and provide them with refreshment,' he ordered. 'They have ridden a long way.'

When Gülbahar and Ahmet had left the room, the young Bey's face grew sad. His eyes clouded and even his golden hair grew dim. He shook himself and rose. He was very tall.

'Sir,' he said, 'the Sheikh's word is our law, but how are we going to carry this through? If it were another man, any other, I would simply ride up to him and say, for my sake give me your daughter Gülbahar to be wedded to my son Ahmet . . . But Mahmut Khan does not speak that tongue. He will have me cast into his dungeon at once. He is an inflexible man, proud and fearless. I know him well. Tell me the whole story now, how it came about that Ahmet abducted the Pasha's daughter from Beyazit Castle, and then we will try to think of something.'

Ibrahim began at the very beginning with the appearance of the horse at Ahmet's door. When he had related everything in detail, the Bey said:

'It's going to be difficult, very difficult. Mahmut Khan must be champing at the bit now. He will not rest until he gets his own back on all of Ararat and Van, and on me too when he knows. By now he must have sent word to the Pasha of Van as well . . .'

All through that night the Bey of Hoshap turned the matter over in his mind.

In the morning he summoned Ibrahim.

'Listen,' he said. 'This is what I have decided. I shall let the matter rest for a fortnight or three weeks. Then I shall send to Mahmut Khan the silver-tongued Molla Muhammet and he will plead our cause. Go to the Sheikh, and tell him that should Mahmut Khan ask for Hoshap Castle in exchange for his daughter, I will give it to him. The army of the Ottomans may march against us, but I will die before I relinquish the girl to anyone. Bear my greetings to my Sheikh and tell him I am grateful for his trust and kiss his hands.'

They had been shown into the room reserved for guests of the highest rank. It had a high ceiling and a marble floor, covered with scarlet felt rugs. The walls were hung with Kurdish *kilims* and rugs of incomparable beauty. The bed was soft and wide and the coverlet of quilted silk.

Gülbahar waited for Ahmet to get into bed first. On the wall a silver oil-lamp was burning. Its tallow had been scented and a heady fragrance filled the room.

Suddenly Ahmet drew out his sword and laid it over the quilt so that the bed was divided into two. The golden hilt glinted icily at the bottom of the pillow. Then, without a word, he stretched himself out on one side of the sword.

Gülbahar was perplexed. Ahmet had done the same thing in the inns and hans of Van and Erjish where they had stopped on the way to Hoshap. This was a sign to say, we sleep in the same bed, you and I, but only as brother and sister. How could he do that, how could their bond ever be that of a brother and a sister? Hadn't she given herself to him, thinking never to meet again? Hadn't she become his woman there in the room above the dungeon of Beyazit Castle? So what was this now? What did Ahmet mean by putting his sword between them?

At last she lay down too. But Ahmet did not kiss her, he did not even touch her . . . The meaning of the sword was clear. They did not exchange a single word.

Gülbahar was sick at heart. What was it? What had happened? Had she offended him in some way or another? Had she, in her ignorance, infringed some old tradition of the Ararat people?

She could not sleep. All kinds of reasons came to her mind, both good and bad. One thing was certain. She could not deceive herself any longer. Ahmet was not the same with her. While she herself was taut as a bowstring and mad with passion, he had grown cold and distant and preoccupied. What was it? Why had he changed?

In the end she could restrain herself no longer. Dawn was about to break. She roused Ahmet.

'Wake up!' she said sharply. 'I have a question to ask

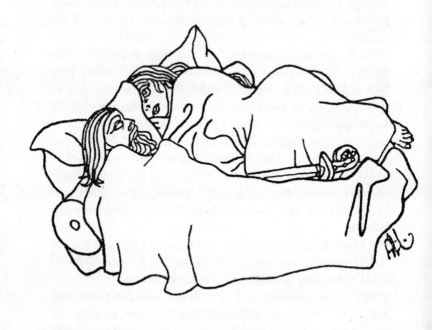

*Gülbahar and Ahmet lying silent, with the
naked sword between them*

you, just one question. And you will answer it truly, straightforwardly, as it is in your heart.'

Ahmet was silent. In the east the mountain peaks were paling. Sunbeams dappled the quilt.

'Why have you placed this sword between us? That is what I want to know. Didn't I become your woman that night in Beyazit Castle? Who ever heard of a sword being laid between man and wife? Or is there some custom, some old tradition among the mountain people of which I am ignorant? Answer me if you love me.'

Ahmet made no reply.

'Speak! Give me a reason,' she insisted.

He could not answer. He was ashamed. The thought that preyed on his mind was so crushing, so terrible, that he strove to chase it away. But in vain . . . How could he tell Gülbahar that searing shameful thing when he could not say it even to himself?

In the end he was forced to lie to her.

'It's not one of our traditions,' he said, 'but of the people of this region, of Hoshap Castle and the surrounding plain . . . That is why I had to put the sword between us. I cannot touch you until your father consents to our marriage.'

Gülbahar was not deceived, but she said nothing more. A vague perception of Ahmet's reason for not touching her flitted through her mind, but she too refused to admit it even to herself.

And so the days passed . . . A worm was gnawing at Ahmet, deep down inside. Gülbahar could see its work of destruction more clearly day by day. Ahmet's eyes were sunken now, dull and lifeless. She too was weakening under this heavy burden. The world had become a dark walled-in place for her. She felt deeply humiliated. Without touching a morsel of food she went about the vast castle of Hoshap like a sleepwalker. Several times a week the Bey of Hoshap would ride out to the hunt. He would take Ahmet with him and they would not return till evening with their bag of wild goats and deer and strange birds. Only on those days could she breathe a little. At least she did not have to watch the agony on Ahmet's face.

Things came to such a pass that Ahmet never even looked at Gülbahar now. Everyone in the castle was aware of this, and so was the Bey. Many times he tried to comfort Ahmet.

'Why do you grieve so, my friend?' he said. 'Even if all the armies of the Ottoman Empire march out against me, I shall see that you get your heart's desire. You have taken refuge in my house. You enjoy the grace of our holy Sheikh, his splendid favour. What has a man like you to fear? How can he let himself sink into despair?'

Ahmet only smiled and never said a word. Nobody must ever know the affliction that racked his heart. Not even Gülbahar. She might guess, but she would never know.

Then one morning, Molla Muhammet who had left for Beyazit a fortnight ago, returned just as the Bey of Hoshap and Ahmet were preparing to go hunting.

The Bey took Molla Muhammet to the Council chamber.

'What news do you bring, Molla?' he asked. 'Good or ill?'

'Ill news,' the Molla replied. His white beard flowed down his breast like a clear stream. 'The Pasha received me very badly. Indeed, he very nearly hacked me to pieces with his sword! Then he said, such disloyalty, such baseness I would expect from anyone but the Bey of Hoshap. Go back to the Bey, he said . . . Tell him to lash those two together with a rope and dispatch them to me at once, with a detachment of soldiers to guard them . . . I shall expect this from the Bey a fortnight from now. If by that time the girl and Ahmet are not here, I shall send my soldiers upon him . . . And he heaped abuse and curses on you, and on the Sheikh too.'

'On the Sheikh? He cursed the Sheikh?'

'Yes Bey, he cursed the Sheikh.'

'He must be mad, raving mad!' The Bey was appalled.

He went out to join Ahmet who was waiting for him at the door, and together they descended to the bridge at the foot of the high fortress. He did not say anything, but Ahmet's eyes were fixed on him so anxiously that at last he turned to him and spoke.

'That Pasha must be quite mad,' he said. 'He dared to curse the Sheikh of the Caravans. It will go ill with him after this. He also threatened to attack us with his army within a fortnight.'

'We must go away, Bey,' Ahmet said. 'Blood will flow because of us. It's not right.'

The Bey bridled.

'You shall not stir from here!' he said. 'No one has ever been known to force Hoshap Castle's gates since it has existed. Mahmut Khan will get a surprise if he decides to attack us. You are a son of this house now. I will never let you go. My whole honour is at stake. This is my

Ahmet and the Bey of Hoshap Castle go hunting

business, not yours. Stay in the castle and don't worry.'

That day, and on the days that followed, the Bey went hunting with Ahmet. But at the same time he was making ready in case of an attack by Mahmut Khan.

From the desert south of Hoshap, from Mount Ararat from as far as Lake Urmiyé in Iran, offers of assistance flowed into Hoshap Castle. Everyone was eager to help the lovers. The Bey was heartened, and proud too. Once again in the history of Hoshap Castle, he would measure himself against the Ottomans. And for a glorious cause too, in defence of the ancient tradition of his fathers, to pay a debt he had taken upon himself.

One day, as the sun was rising, a group of horsemen appeared in the distance, galloping towards Hoshap Castle. All the horses' coats were pure white. The horsemen reined in at the bridge beneath the fortress. The Bey of Hoshap's men greeted them with deference and held the horses' heads.

The Bey himself was waiting to receive them at the gate of the inner rampart. He knew them well, for they were all chiefs of the tribes in the surrounding Hoshap plain. And he knew too why they had come. It meant that Mahmut Khan was not willing to risk a fight.

The Bey of Zilan, young and handsome, brave and dashing, spoke for all. He had a crooked eagle-nose. His voice was deep.

'Bey,' he said, 'let there not be a war because of this affair. We have come to mediate. Mahmut Khan was mustering his army. We held him back. And now it is for you to suggest something.'

In his turn the Bey of Hoshap spoke.

'What can I say that you don't already know?' he said. 'I can never send Ahmet and Gülbahar to the Pasha. That is out of the question. Anything else the Pasha wants of me, I'll do. If I return these two young people now, I and my descendants will be disgraced till the end of time. Even dogs won't look us in the face . . . You are all assembled here, so many Beys. Think of something and I shall abide by your decision. Convey my respects to the Pasha. Tell him I am ready to do anything he wishes, to give up all my possessions, even my life. Let me hold his daughter's wedding and with festivities such as the world has never seen before . . . Let me present his son-in-law with villages and land. Whatever the Pasha wants of me I shall do . . . Only this I cannot do: I cannot, not if it were to save my life, surrender a guest who has sought refuge in my house.'

The Bey of Zilan turned to his companions.

'He has spoken truly,' he said. 'We were wrong to come.'

The others agreed. 'It was wrong of us,' they said. 'If there'd been a spark of manliness in us we would never have put such a dishonourable proposal to the Bey. He has shamed us, and rightly so.'

And on the next day they mounted their horses and rode off.

All this while Mahmut Khan, certain that the Beys would soon be back from Hoshap Castle with the fugitives, was revolving in his mind what tortures he would inflict upon them and what death would be theirs. Never for one moment did he imagine that the Bey of Hoshap would refuse to give them up. After all, the threat still held. He could launch a huge army of Ottoman soldiers against Hoshap Castle and he knew that the Bey was no longer as powerful as he used to be. He would have had second thoughts by now. Others, more powerful Beys than he, had been brought low for much less.

So when the Beys returned to Beyazit empty-handed his anger knew no bounds. He had never expected this. Something was wrong in the land of the Ottomans. Authority was being flouted. He, the representative of the Sultan, was unable to impose his will on a mere Bey . . . He made up his mind to send word to Rüstem Pasha in Erzurum and inform him of the state of affairs. Once he had secured Rüstem Pasha's backing, he would march on Hoshap Castle and raze it to the ground.

He took care not to betray his vexation in front of the Beys.

'The Bey of Hoshap is right,' the chief of Zilan tribe said. 'It is against all tradition to give up two lovers who have sought your protection. Pasha, let us all try to find some other solution.'

Mahmut Khan made no reply.

That day he gave a big banquet in honour of the Beys who had borne his message to Hoshap. His Council chamber was crowded with guests. And the next morning he wrote a long missive for the Pasha of Erzurum.

Rüstem, the Pasha of Erzurum, was a great favourite of the Sultan's. He had spent long years at the court and had been one of the powerful vizirs of his time. Mahmut Khan knew that if the Pasha of Erzurum supported him, the matter would be solved. It would be easy then to have the head of that impertinent Bey of Hoshap.

He couched his missive in terms he thought would best

rouse the Pasha's sympathy, drawing a pathetic picture of the abduction, how one night thousands of people had descended from the mountains like savage wolves, how they had invaded his castle and seized his daughter, how his soldiers had been powerless before that swarming horde.

A long time went by before the messenger returned from Erzurum. Rüstem Pasha had read and re-read Mahmut Khan's missive and had roared with laughter. Then before all the guests at his court that evening, holding his sides and helpless with laughter, he had made the messenger read the letter and tell the story over and over again. The next morning he had dispatched the messenger.

'Give my greetings to Mahmut Khan,' he had told him, 'and bid him give his daughter to that young man without delay. He has deserved her, that young man, as he has deserved the horse. Here is my letter to the Pasha.'

Mahmut Khan read the letter written by Rüstem Pasha himself in his beautiful handwriting and seethed.

'The wretch!' he said. 'The viper! He's making fun of me. If it was his daughter snatched away by some mountain dog, would he laugh and mock like this? Would he mock and ask: Are you going to wage war on all the world because of a girl? The dog! To think I took him for a friend and entertained him in my castle as I would have done the Sultan himself! He was jealous of me, that's it. That's why he wrote this insulting letter. Out of spite . . .'

He read it again and again. He simply could not digest Rüstem Pasha's sarcastic refusal to assist him.

How he longed to send out his soldiers to Hoshap Castle at once! But what if he were defeated? The Bey of

Hoshap was proving someone to be reckoned with. And Hoshap Castle had never before been captured, not since time out of mind.

And so Mahmut Khan chafed and worried, growing more and more uneasy as time passed. Every day he conferred with Ismail Agha. He summoned the Beys he trusted most and consulted with them too. Yet still he could not come to a decision.

All this while silver-tongued Molla Muhammet, the Bey of Hoshap's envoy, came and went to Beyazit Castle.

'Pasha,' he conjured him, 'we are all ready to lay down our lives for you . . . Our Bey begs you not to disgrace him in the eyes of all the world just because of a girl who has run away. I kiss the Pasha's hands, he says, but how can I surrender my guests to him? Nobody, not even the dogs of Hoshap would ever look at me again if I did, nor at any of my descendants either. I am ready to pay the dowry, whatever the Pasha may ask for. Mahmut Khan can take my life . . . I will sacrifice everything for him. And so will Ahmet . . . Ahmet will do the Pasha's every bidding . . .'

Day by day the Bey of Hoshap was kept informed of Mahmut Khan's doings. He knew that he had appealed to the Pasha of Erzurum, the Pasha of Van, and all the Beys of the countryside, and what is more, to the Sultan himself in Istanbul. Sooner or later that stupid obstinate man would move to attack him. He saw it coming. There would be a war that would last for years perhaps. Once again the poor would die of hunger. And all for a girl who had been abducted from her father's house! How had this tradition taken root? In what foolish Bey's head? Among what senseless people?

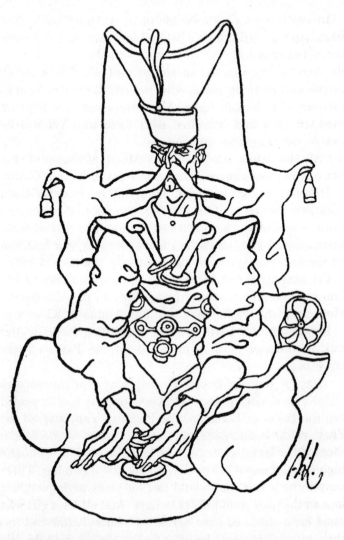

*The march of the people upon Beyazit Castle disturbs
the Ottoman rulers*

In Beyazit the Pasha too had begun to be assailed by fears. An end must be put to this business. The story of the horse, how it had come to stop at Ahmet's door, how its coming had led to a great love, how Memo had sacrificed his life for the lovers, all this combined to lend an aura of sanctity to Ahmet and Gülbahar. One night soon the people of the mountain above and of the plain below would rise up once again. This time they would destroy the castle, leaving not one of its stones standing, nor a single one of its inhabitants alive.

It had become an obsession. He would lie awake at night, on the alert, leaping up at the slightest sound to prowl about the castle, sword in hand, for hours and hours. A cornered man now, the Pasha no longer knew where to turn. His prestige had been damaged and with it the prestige of the Ottomans. He had been forced to knuckle under to that little nobody, the Bey of Hoshap. His defeat was the defeat of the Ottoman Empire.

With every day that passed he wasted away, silent, talking to no one at all now, feeling in his heart a great circle of malediction tightening about him.

* * *

Each year as spring advances over Mount Ararat, the shepherds of the region gather on the shore of Lake Küp, high up on the mountainside. Laying their cloaks over the copper earth at the foot of the red flint-like crags, they sit in a circle all around the lake. Their number is never the same each year. As the east begins to pale, they draw their pipes from their waistbands and begin playing all together the song of Ararat's wrath. And when the day is done they put away their pipes and silently rise to leave. Just at that moment a tiny white bird flutters down, dips one of its wings into the deep blue of the lake, then soars up and flies away. Far up, beneath a great mass of rock that floats like a vessel in the land of snows, a huge horse comes into view, its harness glinting in the twilight. Like a vision it glides above the lake, panting hard, and fades into the plain below.

And in a distant tent a bard kneels down on the crisp singing earth of spring. He takes up his staff and begins his lay. Beside him is a piper who accompanies him on his pipe.

I went down on my knees in the cursed Ahuri Vale, on the earth of a thousand years of love, of a thousand springs, and I called out three times, and three times the mighty mountain answered my call. On my knees I fell, over the verdant earth strewn with flowers of brilliant blue and red and yellow, beneath the twinkling halo of stars clustering about the mountain peak. On my knees on the mountainside, on its snowy breast . . . I knelt before the light and brightness of the mountain that opens its heart to all true lovers . . . And I sang the lay of that awesome wrath. Again I knelt under a dark cloud, in a heady fragrance. A vast torrent of flames rolled down the mountain devouring everything and again I knelt down in its midst. Three times I called out to the mountain, three times I called into the very heart of that earth of a thousand springs, into the ear of this land of a thousand years of love . . . Shepherd, I cried, where are you, shepherd? And the shepherd appeared and stood before me.

Once upon a time a shepherd fell in love with the

daughter of a rich Bey, and she returned his love. The Bey heard of it. He owned fifteen villages, all fifteen of them here, in this cursed Ahuri Vale. Find me that shepherd, the Bey ordered, that miserable wretch who has dared to fall in love with my daughter. I want him dead or alive.

And the bird of love blazed into flames. It built itself a nest of fire in a flaming poplar tree and hatched out its young, three of them. Out they flew one day, the bird of love and its three fledglings of flame. And wherever they alighted the flames flared up. The mountain burst into flame. The stones, the earth, all was aflame. In the sky the stars tossed in a whirlwind of fire. People were burning. Over the mountains and across the seas they went, the love-birds of flame. And the mountains and the far-off places across the sea caught fire and blazed . . . Everywhere the flowers bloomed into flame, bright flames of blue and green and yellow.

The shepherd sought refuge in the mountain. And the heart of Ararat burst into flame. Hot in pursuit the men of fifteen villages were combing the mountain, looking into every nook and cranny, but Ararat was hiding him. The shepherd had become a pillar of flame.

The daughter of the Bey pined for him so, that in the end, she too ran away into the mountain. This time all the people of the fifteen villages, men and women, young and old, flocked out to search for her. But Mount Ararat concealed her too in the flaming fire of its breast.

One day the shepherd, sick with love, begged permission of the mountain to leave his hiding-place.

'I must see my sweetheart once again,' he said. 'If I am to be killed, then so be it.'

*The shepherd lover playing his pipe after having fled into
Mount Ararat from certain death*

And he made his way back into Ahuri Vale. Three days and three nights he roved in the neighbourhood of the village, putting off the moment of death, for death is hard . . . At last, closing his eyes, he walked towards the village. But when he looked again there was nothing and only the wind blew where the houses had once stood. He went to the next village, and the next . . . They had all vanished without leaving a trace. Turning back he came to the tall rock where his home had been, and there he saw his sweetheart wandering desolately through the solitary vale. As the two lovers embraced each other they knew at once what had happened. Angry at all this wickedness and cruelty the mountain had heaved and cast a mass of rock over Ahuri Vale. The fifteen villages with all their living creatures lay buried under this avalanche, swallowed up by the mountain.

The bird of love is a flame. It burns the heart it touches. Its nest is a nest of flames . . . This is the wrath of Ararat, the curse of the mountain. This is how it punishes those who rise against it.

And that is why each spring, as the shores of Lake Küp burst into flower, all the shepherds of Mount Ararat gather at the lakeside . . . They lay their cloaks over the earth of a thousand springs . . . And the flaming bird of love comes to dip its wing into the deep blue of the lake.

*　　*　　*

Hüso the smith, bare to the waist as always, stood at the castle gate, shouting at the top of his voice.

'Pasha!' he roared. 'Pasha! Have you not heard the piper piping the spring? Have you not understood, Pasha,

Hüso the smith entering the Council chamber and
ranting at the Pasha

what that means? The wrath of Ararat be upon you . . .
The curse of Ararat strike you . . . Stop persecuting the
lovers!'

'Go and fetch him in,' Mahmut Khan ordered his men.
'Let's see what he has to say, that smith.'

But when he looked upon Hüso's strong half-naked
body which was like the body of a superhuman being,
Mahmut Khan shivered.

'Did you hear the singer I sent you?' the smith asked
the Pasha.

'I heard him,' Mahmut Khan replied.

'Then what have you to say? Are you not afraid?'

The Pasha was silent.

Hüso lashed out again, saying all that was on his heart.
Then he swung his massive frame and walked off.

'You are warned, Pasha,' he shouted as he went
through the door of the Council chamber. 'Be careful
what you do after this.'

Ismail Agha watched him leave with thoughtful eyes.

'Pasha,' he said, 'I have some questions to put to you.'

'What is it?' the Pasha said.

'Has anyone ever succeeded in climbing to the top of
Mount Ararat?'

'No one,' the Pasha said.

'Could any man of human birth make that climb?'

'Perhaps,' the Pasha replied. 'But even if he did, he
would never come down again. Ararat Mountain would
claim him. It would not let him go.'

Many men had attempted to scale the mountain,
but none had ever been known to return and tell the
story.

A lake of fire burns everlastingly on top of Mount

Ararat, and from its summit a pit descends straight down into the bowels of the earth. It is from this pit that fire was brought upon earth. The first fire that men ever saw was this fire burning in the very heart of Mount Ararat. They saw it, they longed to get hold of it, and they did . . . One day, as the mountain was fast asleep, a man crept up to the lake of fire. Swiftly he tore off a fragment of fire and made fast his escape. Down the slope he ran as fast as his legs would take him. He was nearing the bottom when Ararat awoke and saw the man running away with the stolen fire. At one swoop the arm of the mountain was upon him and he was frozen there on the spot, still holding the burning fire in his hand.

The slopes of Ararat are full of stones and boulders that are the petrified remains of human beings. Mount Ararat has never permitted any mortal to steal its fire. It will never forgive the man who scales its summit and discovers what is there.

'Pasha,' Ismail Agha said, 'I have a suggestion.'

'What is it, Ismail Agha?'

'Let us send word to Hoshap now . . . Let Gülbahar and Ahmet come to Beyazit freely and without fear . . . If you wish I can go and fetch them myself. If Ahmet can climb Mount Ararat and prove to us that he has reached the very summit, then you will give him your daughter, and with your blessing. You will promise to have their wedding here, in Beyazit Castle . . . But if he can't . . . This way we'll be rid of Ahmet. We'll be free of these wagging tongues, of the pressure of people like that smith. Nobody will have anything to say after that.'

The Pasha was very pleased.

'You are right, Ismail Agha,' he said. 'It's a splendid idea. Go to Hoshap yourself, and take a couple of the Beys with you. Make your suggestion, and if Ahmet does not accept, tell the Bey of Hoshap again that he must give up Gülbahar to me, her father.'

Without delay, that very day Ismail Agha and five other men, two of them Beys, rode off for Hoshap Castle.

The Bey greeted them with particular courtesy and held a great banquet in their honour.

That very evening Ismail Agha apprised the Bey of his mission.

'But that's impossible, Ismail Agha!' the Bey exclaimed. 'What you suggest means certain death. The Pasha would be sending Ahmet to his death. What man ever climbed to the peak of Ararat and came back alive? Has anyone ever seen or heard of such a thing?'

'I don't know about that,' Ismail Agha said. 'You told the Pasha you were ready to do anything he suggests. And this is what he suggests.'

'Let us ask Ahmet then,' the Bey said in desperation. 'Let's see what he has to say.'

If Ahmet refused, then the Bey of Hoshap was no longer required to harbour him in his castle. Such were the injunctions of the old tradition, and Ahmet would know this as well as anybody else. Also if the Bey of Hoshap did not comply now, the Pasha would be justified in waging a war against him.

So the Bey sent for Ahmet and put the matter to him in front of Ismail Agha and all the others in the Council chamber.

Ahmet never hesitated for a moment.

'I accept,' he said, his face suddenly eager. 'I will go up to the summit of Mount Ararat and there, in the night, I will light a big fire for the Pasha and everyone to see. Let us make ready to go at once.'

The Bey of Hoshap exhorted him not to embark on this fatal journey. So did Gülbahar and many others in the castle, but Ahmet would not be swayed.

On the second day they bade goodbye to the Bey of Hoshap and rode off, setting their horses' heads for Beyazit.

Ahmet and Gülbahar decided to stop at the house of the Sheikh of the Caravans. The news of their arrival spread like wildfire over Beyazit town and Ararat and through the surrounding countryside. Hüso the smith hastened to their side and together with the Sheikh they tried to dissuade Ahmet.

'That Pasha is an infidel,' they kept saying. 'He wants to see you dead.'

But in vain. Ahmet would not be moved, not even when his people came down from the mountain and begged him not to go.

One morning, having kissed the Sheikh's hand, he rode off to Beyazit Castle and went straight into the Pasha's presence.

'I am going up into the mountain now, Pasha,' he said. 'To scale its summit. I am grateful to you for having set me this difficult task. You were right to do so.'

The Pasha wished him good fortune.

'For three nights, each night you will watch the mountain peak,' Ahmet said. 'On a clear cloudless night a beacon will blaze up there and burn away for all to see.'

Then he mounted his horse once more. The horse

carried him off, up towards the peak of Mount Ararat.

Slowly a crowd began to gather in the town square, in the market-place, in front of the castle . . . People flowed down from the mountain like a slow-moving soundless flood and filled Beyazit town. They moved up from the plain, and the slopes were black with them. The streets, the courtyards, the mosques were full, and still they poured in.

At noontime Ismail Agha came to the Pasha.

'Are they still coming in?' Mahmut Khan asked. 'More of them?'

'More and more,' Ismail Agha said, throwing up his hands in despair. 'Masses and masses of people. There seems to be no end to this human torrent. Who'd ever have thought there could be so many people living hereabouts!'

'Yes, there are many people,' the Pasha said bitterly. 'A great many, but would they ever have got together like this for anything else but mischief? How on earth did they hear so quickly that he was going up the mountain? Who told them? What secret messenger?'

He began to walk up and down his long many-pillared marble chambers, his feet sinking into the thick-piled carpets. His face was sallow and drawn, the wrinkles deeper, and his eyes rolled in their sockets.

He could not help himself. 'Where is she?' he asked. 'That girl . . .?'

Ismail pointed out of the window at the crowd.

'She's over there with the women, on the edge of the

*The multitude besieging the Pasha's castle, more numerous than
the stars in heaven*

crowd, near the tomb of Ahmedi Hani. Look, Pasha, you can see her, dressed in a yellow gown.'

The Pasha turned away, shaking his head. He was going to say something, but he changed his mind and, without looking at Ismail Agha, resumed his pacing up and down. Ismail Agha stood waiting for him to speak. There was a long silence.

Suddenly Mahmut Khan stopped and lifted his head. His eyes smouldered like hot coals.

'Is there nothing we can do, Ismail Agha?' he said. 'No way we can disperse them?'

'We can't do a thing,' Ismail Agha said. 'Our soldiers, the barracks, are completely isolated in a sea of people. They can't move a finger. Here in the castle, we have a bare hundred and fifty or two hundred soldiers. And anyway, it would take many armies such as ours to get the better of such a multitude.'

The Pasha sighed.

'You are right,' he said. 'Go now and see what's happening outside.'

By the evening of that day the throng had swelled to such proportions that it overflowed into the valley below the town, and on to the plain south of the valley. Even the hill above the tomb of Ahmedi Hani was black with people.

And still they came without a break from the mountain and the plain in a never-ending stream. As evening fell tents were put up and fires lit in front of them. Odours of melting butter, dried herbs and cooking mingled with the fragrant scents of spring. Yet this vast immense throng was silent, inert, as though bereft of life, moving like lambent shadows here and there.

It was dark when Ismail Agha returned.

'Are they still coming in?' Mahmut Khan asked him.

'Earth and sky are crawling with people. As countless as the stars in heaven . . . The ground cannot bear them.'

'But I can't hear a sound . . .'

'They're quite silent, Pasha, and still . . . Not even moving their heads to look at the mountain . . . They're just there, a huge multitude, seemingly asleep, as though the earth of the grave had been strewn over them. Not an expression on their faces to show what they're thinking.'

The night was dark, the sky cloudless. The myriad stars seemed nailed to the peak of the mountain and to its slopes. A deathly silence had settled over the town. It was as though that huge crowd were holding its breath.

Mahmut Khan could not sleep. He paced up and down in his silent castle, a prey to black thoughts. To think that so many thousands should come pouring out of the mountain and the plain! All for two lovers? Out of concern for their happiness? That's what it might look like on the surface, but Mahmut Khan sensed much more beneath all this. He sensed anger, an immeasurable anger born of thousands of years of repressed instinctive revolt, a silent dormant anger, ready to find an outlet anywhere, even in the love of a girl and a man. Times are changing, the Pasha thought, and for the worse. The people are getting out of hand. Today they take the pretext of that girl and hold my castle in what amounts to a real siege. Tomorrow, on some other pretext, they will pour into Istanbul city and beset the palace of the Sultan himself. We have reached a turning point and if we don't do something about the people of this land, it will cost us all our heads. To-morrow they'll plead oppression, and the next day it'll be the taxes, and the day after our castles, and after that bread, anything . . . They will gather together in ever greater numbers, the masses, silently like these . . . No force on earth will crush them. Great armies, all the armies in the world will be powerless against such multitudes. Once they band together, nothing will stop them. Something must be done, something, now, to stop this.

The sun rose on a world where the sky was bright and cloudless and the mountain looked clean and shiny. It clung to the mountain ridge, then rose a little; then it touched the ridge again, and finally rose and stayed at the level of the mountain. Mahmut Khan had never seen the sun do that before.

'Even the sun,' he muttered to himself, 'has changed its ways. These are portents . . . Portents of doom . . .'

On leaving the hive the bees toss and turn in the air, hither and thither, and then they find a bough and cluster all over it in a swarm. That was how it was with Beyazit town that morning.

At sunrise a wave of movement passed over the crowd. The men were tall, long-whiskered, wearing motley garments of goat, deer and colt skins and peaked felt caps, and the women were slender-limbed, doe-eyed, dressed in gaudy many-skirted gowns, their coifs of all colours adorned with strings of gold and silver coins.

And still there was no sound.

But by midmorning a change came over the teeming crowds. As one man they turned to face the mountain and, fixing their eyes on the summit, they remained like that, stubbornly unmoving.

Mahmut Khan, aware of this change, was alarmed.

'What's the matter with them, Ismail Agha?' he said. 'Why don't they speak or do something?'

'They're waiting, Pasha. Not even blinking their eyes ... A little while ago I saw them lift up their hands in prayer, but silently. And that was all . . .'

They'll wait here like this a whole three days, Mahmut Khan thought. And then, if they don't see the beacon on the peak of Ararat, they'll turn upon the castle and raze it to the ground, not leaving one stone upon another . . . Or am I imagining things? And frightening myself unnecessarily?

'There are more of them coming, Ismail Agha,' the Pasha observed.

'Yes, more and more . . . Where are they coming from, so many people? Who's bringing them?'

'It's that wretched Sheikh of the Caravans,' Mahmut Khan shouted suddenly. 'That false man of God! Those sheikhs have always been against us, Ismail Agha. If we don't do something to bring them over to our side, then we're lost, lost! Their strength is too deep-rooted, Ismail Agha . . . They have struck root among the people since time immemorial. If we don't make allies of them . . .' He pointed to the crowds from the window. 'Then this is what will happen, Ismail Agha.'

'Pasha, we can have them with us any time,' Ismail Agha said.

Mahmut Khan was thinking. What if I escape tonight,

with my family, my children, my men . . . Leave the castle and go . . . But won't they hear of it in Istanbul? I'll be forever branded as a coward . . . And then, the castle is quite surrounded. How can we get away unobserved? If we fight . . .

Suddenly he exploded.

'Just let me get out of this,' he shouted, 'and I won't rest until I have that Sheikh brought to the block. And the Bey of Hoshap too. I'll have their heads, I will! If it wasn't for them, these people would never have dared to surround my castle like this. I'll have their heads! Their heads, Ismail Agha, you hear? They'll see what I can do. They'll see!'

He was yelling now at the top of his voice, beside himself, his neck-cords swelling thick. On and on he ranted. Then gradually, he calmed down.

'I'll have their heads,' he panted. 'They shan't get away with this.'

Leaning against a pink marble pillar by the door, Ismail Agha waited for Mahmut Khan's anger to abate.

'I can see pipers in the crowd, Ismail Agha. Are there bards too?'

'Hundreds of them Pasha . . . And drummers too. They're making ready for the wedding.'

'Let's hope to God that beacon burns soon on the mountain peak, Ismail Agha. Otherwise . . .'

He stopped, ashamed suddenly at having betrayed his fears to anyone, even to Ismail Agha, his most trusted man. He mumbled something and tried to take back his words. Then he bowed his head.

Ismail Agha was quick to see that the Pasha regretted what he had said. He was a straightforward outspoken man.

'Pasha,' he said, 'if this teeming crowd does not see the beacon on the peak of the mountain tonight, then they'll run amok. They'll raze this castle to the ground and kill us all. Why are we trying to hide this from each other? Why are we afraid to admit it even to ourselves? It is fate, perhaps, but let us do something about it.'

'What?' Mahmut Khan asked eagerly. 'What can we do?'

'You'll give up your demands, Pasha. You'll go out to the castle gate and speak to the people. You'll tell them that for their sake, because so many many people wish it, you have withdrawn your demand. Here, you'll say, for your sake, I give my daughter Gülbahar to Ahmet in marriage. Go and find him and bring him here so we may arrange the wedding. I myself will hold the festivities to please the people of the land and for all to see . . . After this, Pasha, these people will do anything for you. They'll carry you on their heads for ever. You'll be next to God for them . . . It's the only thing to do now.'

'I can't do it, Ismail Agha. Everyone will know I was afraid.'

'Such an idea will never cross their minds. Crowds don't stop to think. They'll be overjoyed.'

'Oh, but it *will* cross their minds, Ismail Agha, it will! A crowd can be shrewd too.'

'No, Pasha, you're wrong. And besides it's not in their interest to attack the castle. They'll be forced to do it, knowing full well what will happen to them after that. If they kill us, it'll be because they've been pushed to it . . . And another thing, Pasha. Ahmet may be dead by now, who knows, engulfed by the angry mountain . . . Perhaps . . .'

142

'No, Ismail Agha,' the Pasha interrupted him. 'I can't do it. You are right, I know. You speak truly, but I can't go back on my word.'

'Pasha, that crowd is afraid. When you announce that you have changed your mind, they'll be so wild with relief and joy it'll never occur to them that you have acted out of fear. On the contrary, they'll make a saint of you, they'll laud your goodness and mercy to the skies. Odes will be sung in your honour.'

'I can't do it, Ismail Agha. I just can't! Let them kill me. And . . . who knows? Perhaps he will reach the summit. Who knows . . . Perhaps we'll see the beacon burn tonight.'

'How can that be?' Ismail Agha cried. 'We all know that the mountain will never let anyone scale its peak. It'll seize Ahmet and turn him to stone, as it has all the others before him.'

'The Sheikh of the Caravans has worked miracles before. Perhaps a miracle . . .'

'Ararat brooks no miracles. It will not allow its sanctity to be violated by any mortal.'

'What if Ahmet does not go right up to the top? What if he lights the beacon somewhere below?'

Ismail Agha stroked his beard. He smiled, rubbed his hands and said:

'He's brave and valiant. When he decided to go he knew it meant death. He won't stop until he reaches the very top.'

'And I'm not a man to go back on my word, Ismail Agha! I'll die fighting. Go, tell the soldiers to make ready. If you can get those at the barracks here, to the castle, then do so quickly. We'll put up a fight before we die.'

143

'We won't have a chance to fight, Pasha,' Ismail Agha objected. 'I've seen crowds like this before. It'll be over with us in the twinkling of an eye.'

'Let it be so then!' the Pasha roared. 'For that twinkling of an eye at least, we'll fight. Go now and do what I tell you.'

Ismail Agha said no more. He knew it would be useless. There was nothing for it but to do the Pasha's bidding.

Evening came and darkness fell. The plain down below the castle was black with people, and more of them kept coming. New tents were erected and fires twinkled all over the plain, star-like.

And as darkness fell the crowd stirred and rose. All eyes were fixed on the mountain peak. As one man, this huge multitude waited, tense, vigilant, for the light that would blaze out on the summit, like a dawning sun.

In his castle Mahmut Khan was waiting too for that same light to burn, waiting with the crowd, his heart in his mouth, for that miracle to dawn on the crest of the mountain.

The midnight cocks crew. And still not a glimmer of light on the mountain save for the stars clustering about its summit. The east began to pale and the dawn-star flashed with a blue radiance whirling upon itself. It shone like a strange, unfamiliar moon, the dawn-star, up there in the paling eastern sky.

Ismail Agha burst into the Pasha's presence. He was sweating.

'They're raising their voices now, Pasha. They're protesting. Some of them are beginning to turn this way, to the castle. Just a few yet, but . . .'

Mahmut Khan's hand went from his sword to the ivory-handled gold-plated flintlock pistol at his waist. It came and went, came and went. All night long his hand had shuttled like this, to and fro. His bloodshot eyes were fixed on the mountain peak.

'Pasha, there's no other way . . . Nothing else can save us . . .'

The Pasha yielded. Swaying heavily, worn out, but summoning his last remaining strength, he walked to the castle gate. In the courtyard, at the door of the mosque, he paused. His feet were dragging him backwards. He longed to return, yet he forced himself forward, until he came to the high-arched, beautifully ornamented Seljuk gate of the castle. The crowd saw him and the angry muttering died away. They stood silent, petrified, not even breathing. For a while Mahmut Khan's huge eyes swept the crowd that heaved like a rolling sea at flood-tide.

Then he climbed on to the mound in front of the castle and addressed them.

'I have pardoned Ahmet for your sake,' he announced. 'And I shall hold his wedding myself. Since you have come here, so many of you, all the people of the land, desiring this . . . I am dispatching my men up into the mountain to bring him back. If there are fleet-footed youths or swift horsemen among you, send them too. Let them find Ahmet and tell him that the Pasha has changed his mind.'

A deep-sounding murmur rose from the multitude and a wave of movement swept it from one end to another. They were like a drawn bow ready to shoot. The Pasha sensed it.

With confident mien, but trembling inside, he de-

*Mahmut Khan addresses the crowd in fear : 'I have forgiven
Ahmet for your sake . . .'*

scended from the mound and with slow steps made his way back through the castle gate. His men followed three paces behind him.

As soon as he had gone, scores of men on horseback and on foot set out for the search, flying swiftly up the slopes of Ararat.

That day the crowd relaxed. People began to talk, and Beyazit town and its environs hummed like a giant beehive. They strolled about lazily under the sun, their hands hanging idly by their sides, aimless, purposeless.

The smith mingled joyfully with the crowd.

'He's been brought to his knees, the infidel!' he exulted. 'Fear brought him to his knees! He knew his golden castle, his marble-pillared sumptuous palace would be razed to the ground. He knew that, friends, and was forced to lick the dust.'

Everyone looked at him with admiration.

'Ah, if we were always like this, united and one in everything,' Hüso repeated, 'no one would ever get the better of us. Even the kings and lords of this earth would give way . . . Just let us stand together, as one man . . .'

There were some who heard him and muttered behind his back. These were people close to the court circle.

'Fire-worshipper!' they said. 'Heretic! What's it to you whether we stand together or not. You're not of our religion, you're just a fire-worshipper!'

Hüso the smith paid no heed to them.

The people camping on the plain were going to and from the town to get the latest news. Already some of them, tired of waiting, had left for their villages and others were preparing to go too. The long wait was over. The tension had relaxed.

Darkness fell once more and the third day ended. The weary discomfited murmur of the crowd grew louder and deeper, as though issuing from the bowels of the earth. Some people, still curious, lifted up their heads now and again towards the summit of the mountain. Mahmut Khan only went to his window once every hour or so.

Only one man kept up the vigil, never took his eyes off the mountain peak, and that was Hüso the smith.

'I have given him my hand,' he prayed. 'Ararat cannot hold him. Ararat will send him back to us. In honour of the holy saints and the sacred fire, Ararat will spare him for us . . .'

And this was the night of the third day. Suddenly, the smith's cry of triumph tore through the darkness. And like a canon-ball exploding, a great booming thundered over the mountain. Ararat swayed and trembled, as loud rumblings reverberated over hill and dale. Everyone looked up and there, on the mountain peak, was a tiny light, glimmering faint and far. It flickered, went out, then shot up again, clear and bright.

Cries of joy filled the night. Drums began to beat and fifes to play. Young girls and youths threw themselves into a mad *gövend* dance. The wedding festivities had begun.

Mahmut Khan summoned Ismail Agha.

'Well?' he said. 'So Mount Ararat was going to seize Ahmet and kill him? What happened?'

'Pasha,' Ismail Agha responded, 'it must be because Ahmet is one of the mountain people. Perhaps the mountain protects its own . . .'

'Nonsense!' Mahmut Khan roared. 'There's more to this business than meets the eye.'

And in the morning Ahmet came galloping down the mountain. He reined in before the castle gate, very straight on the sweat-stained horse. The crowd surrounded him in an instant. They would not let him enter Mahmut Khan's castle, but led him off to the smithy.

He kissed Hüso's hand.

'The holy saints have guarded and aided you,' the smith said. 'May they watch over you like this for ever-more.'

And he blessed him, sending a shower of sparks from the forge over him. Gülbahar had come too and was standing in a corner of the forge. Ahmet never gave her a glance. Deeply hurt, she did not speak to him either.

So this was how it was going to be, she thought. But then why had he risked his life to light that beacon on the mountain peak? She saw it all very clearly now, and anger began to rise in her heart, as great as her love had been.

Ahmet went out and she followed him.

'Let us go,' she said.

'Let us go,' Ahmet said.

They did not enter the castle. They did not look at the crowd. They never saw the gay wedding festivities in their honour. Not even stopping to kiss the Sheikh's hand, they mounted their horses and rode off into the mountain.

*   *   *

Up on the heights of Mount Ararat is a lake no larger than a threshing-floor with waters of a pure deep blue. Each year when spring comes, the shepherds of Ararat gather at this lake just before daybreak. Throwing their cloaks down at the foot of the red crags, they sit in a circle on the

*Gülbahar and Ahmet leaving all behind and going up
into Mount Ararat*

copper earth, on the soil of a thousand years of love, and play on their pipes the song of Ararat's wrath. As evening falls a white bird appears, a tiny white bird. It dips one of its wings into the pure deep blue, soars up again and vanishes. And then a big shadowy horse glides towards the lake, but disappears almost at once. The day has drawn to a close. The shepherds cease playing all at the same time and go their separate ways, fading away into the darkness of the mountain.

*   *   *

They reined in at a cave among the crags overhanging Lake Küp. Tents had been pitched on the plateau above the cave and on the slopes below. Their faint lights dotted the night here and there. There was a pungent, heady scent everywhere, the odour of autumn, sharpening all other smells and lending them the redolence of over-ripe rotting mountain apples. The dry grass, the withered plants, the short, squat bushes rustled in the night breeze.

They tied their horses to a bush. Ahmet struck his flint and busied himself with lighting a fire, while Gülbahar gathered sticks and twigs. Then they sat down facing each other beside the fire. Ahmet took some bread and fragrant green cheese from the saddle-bag. They ate in silence without looking at each other. Now and then, as the fire died down, Gülbahar rose to get more wood. The smoke stung their nostrils but neither of them took any notice of it.

A continuous rumbling rose from a distant gorge and shook the mountain, the thundering echoes of a falling block of ice that had broken off the heights. It was as though not one, but a hundred avalanches were crashing down at the same time. At all seasons these avalanches occur on Mount Ararat. Huge masses of ice, each one a mountain in itself, roll down the gorges and ravines, raising even louder echoes.

Gülbahar was huddled with her chin on her knees, a tiny ball. Outside the cave, a storm came and went, leaving a frosty tang in the air, which softened again almost at once. It was past midnight, and still they sat like that face to face, not moving, their eyes fixed on the burning fire.

They could not bring themselves to speak. But Gülbahar's resentment was growing stronger. As deep-rooted as her love had been, anger lashed at her heart, uncontrolled.

'Speak, Ahmet,' she burst out at last. 'Something is rankling in you. Say it.'

Ahmet's large eyes widened in amazement, as though he had only just become aware of her presence, as though she were someone he had known very long ago and had not seen for years. He seemed to be making an effort to remember who she was. That was how he was looking at her.

He did not know what to say. Gülbahar's voice was like a devastating fire and he had to answer her. His eyes were on her face.

When he spoke the words came slowly, like the hard agony of death.

'How did you save me, Gülbahar? What did you give Memo in exchange for my life? For what did Memo sacrifice himself to save me? He knew, didn't he, when he set me free that it meant death for him? Tell me this, did he know or not?'

He looked straight into her eyes and waited.

'He knew,' Gülbahar replied. 'No jailer who opens wide the doors of a prison can expect mercy or survival here or anywhere in the world. Memo knew this. That is why he chose to die fighting, that is why he flung himself down from the bastion of the tower.'

'Did you offer him gold to risk his life?'

'No.'

'Did you present him with rich palaces, that he was tempted?'

'No.'

'What did you give him then, Gülbahar, what price for my life? How is it he sacrificed his life for mine?'

'I gave him nothing, Ahmet,' she said. 'He never asked for anything.'

'Nothing in exchange for my life?'

Gülbahar stopped him.

'I told him,' she said, 'that I was ready to give him anything he wanted in exchange for your life. He asked for nothing.'

'You told him you would give him whatever he asked of you, is that so?'

'I said I would give him anything he wanted,' she said again. 'And he never asked for a single thing.'

They fell silent.

The fire was slowly dying out. For Gülbahar everything was over. She knew now exactly what Ahmet was accusing her of.

He rose, took the felt saddle-cloth from the horse and made a bed of grass on the ground. The strong-scented heather he stacked as a pillow. He unsheathed his sword and laid it in the middle of the bed. In the light of the dying fire the sword gleamed dully. Then he lay down drawing the saddle-cloth over his body.

Gülbahar went out and returned with another armful of brushwood. The fire flared up and she looked upon Ahmet's face with adoration, with a hungry yearning. She could never have her fill of looking at him, and the more she looked the more her love swelled, intensifying her despair. It was over . . . Everything was lost, gone for ever . . . The realization struck at her heart with a stabbing pain. She could not bear it. What was she to do now? Where should she go? With whom could she find shelter? She was steeped in love to the very marrow of her bones. Was it possible that this love of hers was not true and pure? Should she have let Ahmet go to his death if she had truly loved him, rather than . . .? And Memo . . .?

She went out of the cave, swaying on her feet. The stars tossed and dropped over the mountain, then swirled up again. Mount Ararat rose and fell and whirled in a seething mass in unison with the stars. The mountain thundered, shook, rumbled and crashed down. Gülbahar staggered into the cave with another armful of brushwood. The fire blazed and Ahmet's face grew even more beautiful, more full of love.

Was he asleep? In an ecstasy of love? Or just tired to death? Gülbahar felt as if she were choking. Her eyes were on Ahmet, on his face that was growing more and more beautiful as she looked. The flames leaped and blazed and spread. Gülbahar writhed in pain. The world whirled all around her, the rocks about the cave split with terrifying cries. Outside the stars were hurtling through the sky in a

154

boiling ferment. The world rocked with a terrifying thundering sound; the whole of nature was in chaos.

Suddenly Gülbahar was engulfed in darkness. And in that darkness only Ahmet's face was clear and bright. Her hand went to her dagger. It struck again and again, where, she did not know, ceaselessly it struck until her arm fell back tired.

When she opened her eyes the first light of dawn was filtering into the cave. The air was warm, bearing sharp fragrant scents.

And then, in a blaze of light, she saw Ahmet lying on a rock half buried in darkness.

She threw herself at him.

'Ahmet! Ahmet! Come to me Ahmet . . . Ahmet, Ahmet, Ahmet!'

Her cry echoed all over Mount Ararat. It set avalanches tumbling down through the gorges and ravines. The mountain was shaken to its very heart.

Ahmet was drawing away from her. The more she went after him, the farther away he drifted. When she stopped he stopped too, but as soon as she walked to him, he receded into the distance. Down to the shores of Lake Küp they went, and there Gülbahar lost sight of him. She sank down on the copper earth beside the lake and rested her head in her hands. There, she remained motionless, her eyes fixed on the deep blue waters of Lake Küp.

From that day to this, passers-by may see her there, sitting by the lakeside, her long dark hair flowing down her back like a flood of light. She holds her head in her

*Each year as spring breaks into flower the white bird comes
to dip its wing into the deep blue of Lake Küp*

hands and her eyes never move from the deep-blue waters. Sometimes, under the surface of the lake she catches sight of Ahmet. Swiftly she stretches out her arms and walks to him.

'Ahmet, Ahmet!' she cries, and her voice resounds all over Mount Ararat. 'Ahmet, Ahmet! You would have done the same if you had been in my place. Oh, it's enough! Enough! Come to me, Ahmet! Ahmet, Ahmet . . .'

The lake ripples and Ahmet's face vanishes . . . Gülbahar vanishes too, and a tiny white bird swoops down and dips its wing into the deep blue of the water. And afterwards, the dark shadow of a horse falls over the surface of the lake and fades away.

*　　*　　*

Each year, as spring breaks into bloom and the world begins to sing, shepherds from all over Mount Ararat come to the lakeside. They cast their felt cloaks over the copper earth surrounding the lake and sit in a ring on the earth of a thousand years of love. As dawn glimmers in the east they draw out their pipes and play the song of Ararat's wrath and of its passion. And as the day draws to its close, the white bird appears . . .